You Must Remember This...

SONGS at the Heart *of the* War

A nation's music belongs to the race
Through the slow time changes,
And the rhythm of moving years,
Our nation's songs are its pride and its grace
Evermore and after.
Though the shape of the world may alter,
In our songs the laughter
Blends the tears,
From the past
We hear the echo of songs that proved us free
They are bequeathed to you and me
Forever and ever.

– Noël Coward (*There Have Been Songs in England*)

You Must Remember This… is the companion book to the
BBC television programme 'You Must Remember This…' produced
by Café Productions Ltd and Big Ben Entertainments Ltd.

You Must ★ Remember This...

SONGS at the Heart of the War

Foreword by
Bill Cotton, Jnr

BOXTREE

Steven
SEIDENBERG
★
Maurice
SELLAR
★
Lou
JONES

Acknowledgements

The authors would like to give their special thanks and acknowledgements to Anne Morrison, Claudia Rosencrantz, Jane Plackett and Steve Nam (BBC); Caroline Underwood and Tracy Cousins (Warner Chappell Music); Mick Booth (Noel Gay Music Co. Ltd/Campbell Connelly and Co. Ltd); Steve Clark (International Music Publications Ltd); Richard Dinnadge, Alison Wenham and Michael Kennedy (Conifer Records); Robert Bruce (Bodleian Library, Oxford); Cy Payne; Phil Farlow; Arthur Knight, Robyn O'Brien, George Marshall. To Katy Carrington and Anita Ruddell at Boxtree, our warmest thanks; and most of all, thanks to our colleagues at Café Productions and Big Ben Entertainments without whose support neither the film nor this book would ever have been made.

Special Edition for PAST TIMES®, Oxford, England

First published in Great Britain in 1995 by Boxtree Limited.
Text © Steven Seidenberg, Maurice Sellar and Lou Jones 1995.

PHOTO CREDITS: **Hulton Deutsch** (9–13, 15, 16, 18, 20, 21 bottom, 25, 26, 30, 33, 35–40, 41 left, 42 bottom, 43, 45, 47, 48, 52 bottom, 54, 56, 59 bottom, 60, 65, 66, 68, 70–78, 79, 81, 83, 84 top, 85–87, 89, 93, 97, 101, 106 right, 108, 110, 112, 113 bottom, 117, 118–123, 124, 125 top, 126, 127, 128 left, 129, 130, 131 right, 132 top, 133; **Popperfoto** (59 top, 102, 106 left, 107, 115, 116, 129 bottom, 130, 131 left); **Kinema Collection** (103, 104, 125 left, 128 right, 131 right, 132 right, Colour section – 6–8); **Imperial War Museum** (19 bottom, 51, 52 top, 57, 63, 64 right, 82, 84 top, 95, Colour section – 1–3); **Range/Bettmann/Springer** (62, 90, 113 top, 115); **Warner Chappell Music Ltd, London W1Y 3FA (reproduced by permission of IMP Ltd)** (14 right, 17, 31, 41 right, 55, 64 left, 80, 84 bottom, 91, 92, 99, Colour section – 4 top and bottom, 5 top and bottom); **Noel Gay Music Co. Ltd/Campbell Connelly and Co. Ltd** (14 left, 21 top, 29, 34, 99, Colour section – 4 middle, 5 middle); *Evening Standard* (42 top, 53); *Daily Express* (27 top); **Topham** (title page, 19 top, 24, 27 bottom, 46, 88, 132 bottom).
For copyright holders of all lyrics quoted in this book, please refer to the song index on pages 140–143.

Book and jacket design by Anita Ruddell.

Printed and bound in Great Britain by Butler and Tanner, Frome, Somerset for:
Boxtree Limited
Broadwall House
21 Broadwall
London SE1 9PL

A CIP catalogue entry for this book is available from the British Library.

ISBN: 0 7522 1065 3

Contents

Foreword ☆ 6
by Bill Cotton, Jnr

Foreword

I WAS TEN YEARS OLD when war broke out. Over the previous ten years I had been brought up to a marked degree in the world of popular music. My father had started as a bandleader working in dance halls and later changed the Billy Cotton Band into a show band working in the theatres, both in variety and Sunday concerts. He also had a recording contract and frequently broadcast both on the BBC and Radio Luxembourg.

I had got to know the great names in songwriting and publishing like Noël Gay, Lawrence Wright, Jimmy Campbell and Reg Connelly. It was an exciting world full of laughter and fun, and like a lot of people I can still remember the words of songs I learned in those days.

The advent of war sounded a more serious note. Like any child of ten at the time, a lot of the concern went over my head; but both my father and mother had lost a brother in the 1914–18 Great War and that had only been twenty years before. In common with everyone else of their generation, they had heard the 'it will be over by Christmas' story before.

The Phoney War dragged on and the Cotton Band went to France with ENSA to entertain the troops, armed with *We're Gonna Hang out the Washing on the Siegfried Line* and other jingoistic songs reckoned to keep everyone's morale up. On coming back from France, the band continued working the variety theatres and broadcasting on radio. Changes in the band were inevitable as men were called up or volunteered to go into the services and war work.

The war, which had already become a reality in Czechoslovakia and Poland, then struck the French army and the BEF serving in France. It was short, but not sweet. Songs like *The Last Time I Saw Paris* captured the spirit of the time and Hughie Charles, a great friend of the family, co-wrote one of the most inspirational songs of the war, *There'll Always Be An England*, which, although it didn't go down too well with the Scots and Welsh, was an enormous hit in this country and supplied my father with a *finale* for his show for years.

Then came the Blitz. For all variety performers, including the Cotton Band, this became a game of Russian Roulette – there was a time when we thought the Germans had got a copy of the band's concert-date book. When they were in Birmingham, bombs demolished the old Bull Ring; on the Thursday of the same week they played Plymouth, my mother was blown on to the stage by the blast of a bomb that destroyed the pub next to the theatre. At Bristol, the studio was hit and the band lost most of their instruments and their music library. Coventry and Glasgow were among the many other towns visited by the Luftwaffe during the week of the appearance of 'Britain's Brightest Band' (as the Cotton Band was billed).

Foreword

To add insult to injury, the only bomb that landed in the Blackpool area during the war – you've guessed it – dropped when my father was playing the Opera House. Despite all this, the band played on and the audiences were terrific. If there was a raid, when the show finished they stayed in the theatre and had a singsong – *Run, Rabbit, Run!*, *Roll Out the Barrel*, *We'll Meet Again* – there was no shortage of good songs, and singsongs happened at the drop of a hat, often at the most desperate times and in the most disparate places.

One such song was *Lili Marlene*. Of a Sunday evening, the Cotton family used to bicycle over to a nearby pub called the Dog and Pot. One Sunday, some troops of the 51st Highland Division, fresh back from North Africa, were in the pub and started to sing this haunting melody. As we sat and listened, it became clear that the words they had written to it were not suitable for the broadcasting of the day, but thanks to the subsequent collaboration of one of Britain's top lyricists, Tommie Connor, and one of my father's friends, music publisher Jimmy Phillips, a respectable lyric was produced – and an instant hit.

Then the Americans came and with them nylons, fried chicken, Lucky Strike cigarettes, bubble gum and a whole lot of music. Glenn Miller's band of the AEF (formerly the AAF) brought with them a sense of musical precision that was the envy of the British music profession.

In London, bands in the night-clubs were playing *A Nightingale Sang in Berkeley Square*, *These Foolish Things,* and the theatres were full of laughter and music. Sid Field was a hit at the Prince of Wales Theatre in the show, 'Strike A New Note'. It featured a song sung by Zoë Gail, *We're Going to Get Lit Up (When the Lights Go Up in London)*, which reflected the optimism of the day as much as the song *Spring Will Be A Little Late This Year* reflected the sadness of innumerable partings.

One final assault on Britain from the air came with the V1s and V2s late in 1944. Just when everything seemed to be looking up, these devilish unmanned devices were launched on us. (At first, we thought they were targeted but soon realized they were indiscriminate.) At that time, my father had an office in the building in Denmark Street, known as Tin Pan Alley, that belonged to Noel Gay. One day, the warning blew. Everyone was meant to go straight to the cellar, but Noel Gay and my father decided instead to get into a cupboard on the third floor – a floor which had no windows, so flying glass would not be a problem. As they were settling down inside, the door opened and to their shame an eighteen-year-old secretary served them with tea.

From D-Day to VE-Day the music of the two nations combined to entertain both the troops overseas and the people at home. The BBC was

augmented by the AFN (American Forces Network) and brought a new kind of entertainment to the British scene – disc jockeys who played records on the radio all day. (There was one programme I remember well which started with the DJ saying 'Here it is, men - Dufflebag'.)

All in all, the popular music of the day was a great comfort to many people in many different circumstances. This book captures the breadth and effect of these songs, which had the power to make you feel sad, proud, defiant or jolly, depending on your situation. To those of us who remember it, the music, like the records, truly goes round and round – probably for the rest of our lives.

This well illustrated book certainly evokes the musical mood of the time, and many of the songs featured are a nostalgic reprise for me.

'You Must Remember This...'? – Yes, I do, with great pleasure.

BILL COTTON, JNR
London, March 1995.

CHAPTER ONE

The Last Summer

One Day When We Were Young

I T WAS A BEAUTIFUL summer. The summer of 1939 was one of the hottest and driest on record. The sun shone like there would be no tomorrow and people pushed thoughts of war far from their minds. In the London parks night-time dances were held that attracted people in their tens of thousands. And the popular songs of the day gave little hint of the horror to come. Deanna Durbin scored a hit with *One Day When We Were Young* while Ella Fitzgerald wowed them with *Chew-Chew-Chew Your Bubble Gum*. People lived for the day, and sang *Heaven Can Wait* while the tone-poem *Deep Purple* topped the charts. But the echo of the rumbling war clouds could, perhaps, also be heard as they listened to such songs as *My Prayer* and *And the Angels Sing*.

> *We meet, and the angels sing*
> *The angels sing the sweetest song*
>   *I ever heard*
> *You speak and the angelas sing*
> *Or am I reading music into*
>   *every word*

CHAMBERLAIN'S SHORT-LIVED SUCCESS AT MUNICH INSPIRED NOT ONLY THIS TRIBUTE, BUT AN EVEN SHORTER-LIVED SONG.

For a short time it appeared that the British Prime Minister, Neville Chamberlain, had performed a miracle. In his emotional return from his 1938 meeting in Munich with the German

Chancellor, Herr Hitler, he clutched a scrap of paper and proclaimed that we would enjoy 'peace in our time'. It seemed as if the policy of appeasement had paid off and a grateful nation breathed easier. A wonderful, if little-known, song called *God Bless You Mr Chamberlain* commemorated his success.

> *God bless you Mr Chamberlain,*
> *For deeds we can't forget.*
> *You look swell holding your umbrella,*
> *All the world loves a wonderful fella.*

A year later, however, after the Nazi invasion of Poland, Mr Chamberlain's stock plummeted and the song quietly disappeared for the duration.

The hopes raised in 1938 were short-lived. In March 1939, the Czech President Emil Hacha succumbed to German pressure and 'voluntarily' signed away Czech territory. Without firing a shot the Germans had destroyed the most progressive and democratic state in Central Europe. Not satisfied, less than a week later Hitler made new territorial demands: this time he wanted Memel from Lithuania and Danzig (Gdansk) from Poland. The die was cast for war.

Ironically, one of the most famous songs of the whole war was borrowed from the Czechs at almost the precise time that their country was being sold down the river. *Roll Out the Barrel (The Beer Barrel Polka)* was originally published in Czechoslovakia in the early Thirties. In May 1939, Lew Brown put new

TWO DAYS AFTER HITLER MARCHED INTO POLAND, BRITAIN AND FRANCE DECLARED WAR ON GERMANY.

words to Wladimir Timm and Jaromir Vejvoda's original Czech version and this jolly, up-beat song was soon repeated the length and breadth of Britain. Easy to remember, its cheerful words and catchy tune helped to keep up people's spirits in times of trouble.

The Last Summer

Roll out the barrel,
We'll have a barrel of
fun.
Roll out the barrel,
We've got the blues
on the run.

Roll Out the Barrel was sung by drunks staggering back home through the blacked-out streets and, later, by civilians as they were pulled from the ruins of their blitzed homes. There were even reports of its being sung by sailors as they awaited rescue from their torpedoed ships.

There were many alternative versions of the song. As the war dragged on, a common variation was the substitution of the word 'Hun' for 'blues' in the last line. Another version praised the armed forces:

Roll out the army,
Roll out the navy as well.
Roll out the air force,
We'll bomb old Hitler to hell.

Yet that was all in the future, for the summer of 1939 was spent in peace. The expected war did not materialize. Even after the disastrous events in Czechoslovakia the *Daily Mirror*'s gossip columnist, Charles Graves, noted that 'the jitters seem now to have almost entirely disappeared'. The *Tatler*, never an organ

CROWDS GATHERED
IN DOWNING STREET ON THE DAY
WAR BROKE OUT.

completely in touch with the real world, refused to let anything spoil the fun. An April 1939 headline unambiguously proclaimed: 'On with the Fun, and Blow the Axis!'

One of the best places to have fun in that heady summer was in one of the many ballrooms across the nation. One of the popular dances of the period, the Paul Jones, was danced to the song *Here We Go Gathering Nuts in May*. In this dance, concentric circles of men and women rotated around the floor until a pause in the music brought them face to face with a new partner. The Lambeth Walk, already popular from the 1937 smash hit musical 'Me and My Girl', became even

You Must Remember This...

more popular during the war, as did other old favourites the hokey-cokey, the conga, and the palais glide (in which friends and strangers linked their arms and kicked their legs in time to the music). Annette Mills (sister of John Mills – star of so many stiff-upper-lip wartime British movies and later better known as the creator of TV's first great puppet success Muffin the Mule) introduced a new novelty dance, Hands, Knees and Boomps-a-Daisy which became a favourite at community dances every-where. As the war progressed, novelty and community dances such as these pro-liferated. The Blackout Stroll was intro-duced during the Phoney War period (September 1939–April 1940), while the Kangaroo Hop commemorated the arrival of Australian troops. The great popularity of these community dances may well be found in the fact that unlike the tango or its successor, the jitterbug, these novelty dances could be performed by even the most Terpsichorially-challenged.

Yet not everyone dallied on the dance floors. For cooler heads the signs were clear and the summer of 1939 saw their continuing preparations for the inevitable war. Buildings were sand-bagged and trenches were dug across city parks while the combined efforts of the Women's Voluntary Service, the Red Cross and the Boy Scouts distrib-uted some 38 million gasmasks in the months preceding the declaration of war.

There was a flurry of anti-Hitler songs in the years leading up to the war as well as during the war itself. Most were fairly mild, although even so, in 1936 the fainthearted BBC managed to ban *Even Hitler Had a Mother*. The spirit of appease-ment apparently extended to the fear of wounding the tender feelings of the German Chancellor.

(*LEFT*): SONGWRITER ANNETTE MILLS FOUND TELEVISION FAME AFTER THE WAR WITH 'MUFFIN THE MULE'.

(*BELOW*): NEAR ROTTEN ROW, IN HYDE PARK, TRENCHES WERE DUG – TO THE CONSTERNATION OF COURTING COUPLES.

Even Hitler had a mother,
Even Adolf had a ma.
Although we may suffer for
*   his blinkin' sins,*
At least, thank Gawd, he wasn't
*   twins.*

With the outbreak of war there was a rush to publish anti-Hitler songs. In this belt-tightening, bracing-for-the-onslaught Britain, they proliferated. Songs of derision were chorused in the music halls and whistled in the streets. One such song was *Adolf*, also written by Annette Mills. The lyric had a middle-class-naughty-schoolboy approach – unsurprisingly, as the Mills' father had been the headmaster of a public school.

> *Come on, hold your hand out,*
> *We're all fed up with you*
> *   – cor blimey!*

Other songs that poked fun at Hitler included *It's Just Too Bad for Nasty Uncle Adolf, Who is That Man Who Looks Like Charlie Chaplin?*, and *Old Man Schicklegrüber.*

None, however, had any lasting success owing, perhaps, to the disastrous turn of events on the battlefield in 1940 and 1941. These years of defeat and retreat, of Dunkirk, Tobruk, Hong Kong and Singapore, were not conducive to jocular songs and it was not until much later in the war, after the Allied victories at El Alamein and Stalingrad, that full rein was again given to anti-Hitler feelings. Today these songs, and others of the same ilk such as Ronald Frankau's *The Jap and the Wop and the Hun,* or *Even Hitler Had a*

Mother, would be seen as seriously politically incorrect, but at the time they provided an essential outlet for the pent-up frustrations of the nation.

By far the most successful of the second-generation anti-Hitler songs was *Der Führer's Face,* written by Oliver Wallace to be sung in cod-German accents. Its topical references to the Nazi ('nut-sy') leaders was enormously appealing. 'Ve iss der Master Race', 'Ve own der Vorld und Space', 'Dey'll neffer bomb dis place', all accompanied by the raucous blowing of 'raspberries' (or 'Bronx cheers' as the Americans call them) not only in the Führer's face, but also those of his henchmen, Goering and Goebbels, for good measure.

> *Vee Heil!* (razz)
> *Heil!* (razz)
> *Right in der Führer's face.*

The uproarious rudery of *Der Führer's Face* was immediately infectious on both sides of the Atlantic as the impudent everywhere adopted mock German accents and blew raspberries in der Fuehrer's face. So popular was the song that it was covered by many leading recording artists including Tommy Trinder in Britain and Spike Jones in America. Even the normally conservative Walt Disney got in the act, with a cartoon version featuring Donald Duck.

The Disney Studios were active throughout the war years, coming up with some of their most memorable products. Not only did they make several of the most beloved feature-length cartoons of all time during the war – 'Pinocchio', 'Fantasia', 'Dumbo', and 'Bambi' – but they also produced several shorts that were dedicated specifically to help the war effort – *The Three Caballeros, Der Führer's Face, Victory Through Airpower* – as well as numerous training and information films for the armed forces.

The London opening of 'Pinocchio' coincided almost exactly with the start of the war, which may help to explain why three of its songs (*When You Wish Upon a Star, Give a Little Whistle,* and *I've Got no Strings*) topped the music charts in May 1940. But the biggest morale-booster of all must surely have been their version of *Der Führer's Face* in which Donald Duck had a nightmare vision of life as a soldier in Nazi Germany, and with his characteristic short fuse heiled (razz), heiled (razz) right in der Führer's face.

As the Walt Disney cartoon 'Snow White and the Seven Dwarfs' had been released shortly before the war, this film too was still fresh in people's memories. So it is not surprising that children produced their own parody lyrics to its songs. The song *Whistle While You Work* had many variants.

Whistle while you work.
Hitler is a twerp.
He's half barmy,
Join the army,
So whistle while you work.

Another version was more nonsensical:

Whistle while you work
Mussolini bought a shirt,
Hitler wore it,
Musso tore it,
So whistle while you work.

From songs such as these it is clear that even the youngest children knew who the enemy was.

There were, of course, dozens of songs whose lyrics underwent radical transformation in the barrack-rooms. Perhaps none was more famous than the *Colonel Bogey March* theme. Although now best remembered as the theme from David Lean's 1957 film 'The Bridge On The River Kwai', the wartime version of the song began with the unforgettable line 'Hitler has only got one ball'.

Hitler has only got one ball.

Goering has two, but very small.
Himmler has something similar,
But poor old Goebbels
Has no balls at all.

Other songs were even more boisterous and vulgar. *The Bells of St Mary's* was re-versioned to have a dig at the bane of the squaddies' existence, the Sergeant Major.

The balls of Sarn't Major are wrinkled
and crinkled,
Capacious and spacious as the dome of
St Paul's.
The crowds they do muster
To gaze at the cluster,

TWO PINTS LESS FOR THIS SHOP OWNER, CALLED UP ON HER MAJESTY'S SERVICE.

You Must Remember This...

They stop and they stare
At that glorious pair
Of Sarn't Major's balls
Balls, balls, balls, Balls, balls, etc.

Sadly, government regulation (and native good taste) meant that none of these songs ever graced the airwaves. Nevertheless, they remained popular in pubs, barracks and schoolyards across the country.

However, that glorious last summer jingoistic songs got fairly short shrift. Most people rejected sabre-rattling, perhaps as a way of denying the inevitable. The most popular songs were those of simple good cheer or else, like Georges Boulanger and Jimmy Kennedy's *My Prayer*, of contemplative hope for the future.

My prayer
And the answer you give,
May they still be the same
For as long as we live.

OFF TO NEW HOMES, THE EVACUEES TURN THEIR BACKS ON THE BIG CITY, TAKING THEIR TRUSTY GAS MASKS WITH THEM.

CHAPTER TWO

The Call to Arms

Wish Me Luck as You Wave Me Goodbye

THE GERMAN INVASION of Poland on 1 September 1939 marked the end of that carefree last summer. For the next six years the world was caught up in the greatest war in history. By its end, more than 18 million soldiers and 20 million civilians would be dead, whole cities destroyed, whole nations in ruins. The invasion of Poland ended the false calm and complacency of the summer of 1939. September brought a burst of activity both in the military and on the home fronts. The battle cry had sounded and it was answered by a massive call to arms.

Throughout the war there was a never-ending stream of songs to encourage men to enlist in the armed forces. A variety of strategies was used – patriotism, shame, enjoyment, adventure – but one of the most effective employed the opposite sex for bait. Innumerable songs stressed the irresistibility of a man in uniform or told how women loved a soldier. Mack Gordon and Harry Warren's *You*

Can't Say 'No' to a Soldier (or a Sailor or a Handsome Marine) sent a clear message to those thinking about volunteering for the services.

So get out your lipstick and powder...
Oh you can't say 'no',
You've gotta give in,
If you want him to win for you.

MUSICAL STARS
BEA LILLEY (*LEFT*) AND 'BOO'
(EVELYN) LAYE OPEN A ROYAL NAVY RECREATION
HALL AT ROSYTH, SCOTLAND.

In *A Pair of Silver Wings* by Eric Mashwitz and Michael Carr, it is an air force man who gets the girl. After she says that no matter how tough his job is, she wouldn't have him trade it for the King's, the song continues:

I'm so full of pride when we go walking
Every time he's on leave,
He with those wings on his tunic,
Me with my heart on my sleeve.

Although it would be another two years before America joined the war, Dale Evans (who appeared with Glenn Miller in the film 'Orchestra Wives' and who later married singing cowboy Roy Rogers) expressed a similar sentiment in *I'm in Love With a Guy Who Flies in The Sky*.

Of course it was not only airmen who got the girls. The senior service had its own special songs. *All Over the Place*, by Noel Gay and Frank Eyton, was such a jaunty homage to the sailor's life that it could almost have been written by recruiting officers. Its lyric describes a woman's true love for a sailor, whose life, she says, is 'much more exciting than a tinker's or a tailor's'. The lyric goes on to hint at the other rewards a roving sailor could expect.

The ladies adore
To get him ashore,
He's theirs for a day,
And then he's away.

Del Beeman and Jay Johnson's *My Heart Belongs to a Sailor* expresses a similar sentiment.

Oh my heart belongs to a sailor,
Who sails the wide blue sea.
My heart belongs to a sailor,
I hope his belongs to me.

The female lead of Redd Evans' American ditty *Gobs of Love* clearly indicated a similar preference for a boy in blue.

Though my heart skips a beat
When a soldier I meet
What it won't do
When I see a man in blue.

Here I am, Uncle Sam

Although the United States didn't join the war until December 1941, once they did so there was a flood of recruiting songs. Their titles provide a clear indication of the range of emotions that were played upon as young men were encouraged to enlist in the armed forces: *Fall In, The Conscription Waltz, Charlie, Brother There's a Job to Do, First Call, Fighting Men of Uncle Sam, Four Buddies, Here I Am Uncle Sam, I Want to Be A Soldier, I'd Die for the Red, White and Blue, If Mother Could See Me Now, I'm Proud of My Boy*, and, of course, the greatest flag-waver of them all, the classic *Yankee Doodle Dandy*.

However, in Lyle Moraine and Chuck Foster's *I've Been Drafted (Now I'm Drafting You)*, the recruitment cut both ways.

> *My country called me to do my part,*
> *My country needs me and I need you*
> *   sweetheart.*
> *I want someone whose heart will*
> *   volunteer*
> *To wait for me at least another year.*

Having answered the call, the volunteer had to pass a rigorous physical examination before he could become a soldier. *He's 1-A in the Army and He's A-1 in My Heart* celebrated this fact before continuing with the ultimate emotional blackmail:

> *I love him so*
> *Because I know*
> *He wants to do his part.*

The '1-A' mentioned in the song refers to the US Draft Board classification scheme. 1-A, the top classification, meant fit for immediate military service. At the other end of the scale, the category 4-F (immortalized by Danny Kaye's scat song, *Melody in 4F*, about the induction of a hypochondriac into the army) indicated that the candidate was not fit for service and should be immediately discharged. Other songs that made fun of the induction process included *Melody in 1-A* and *Bring Enough Clothes (for Three Days)*.

There were even cowboy songs about the call to arms. *I'll Be Back in a Year, Little Darlin'*, written by Ben Shelhamer, Claude Heritier and Russ Hull and performed by the singing cowboy Red Foley, had great success in America – even if, as with US involvement in the First World War, the composers underestimated the likely duration of the fight.

> *I'll be back in a year, little darlin',*
> *Uncle Sam has called and I must go.*
> *I'll be back, don't you fear, little darlin',*
> *You'll be proud of your soldier boy,*
> *   I know.*

'THE DAY OF INFAMY': PEARL HARBOR, 7 DECEMBER 1941.

BAND LEADER GERALDO BROADCASTING TO THE TROOPS

Nor are we left in any doubt as to the feelings of the girls at home in Ira Schuster, Paul Cunningham and Leonard Whitcup's *I Wanna Dance With A Sailor*. With a penchant for 'salt water kisses' and a thrill for the arms of the navy, the songstress makes her feelings plain as she sings:

> *I wanna dance with a sailor,*
> *I wanna dance with a gob …*
> *I love those salt water kisses,*
> *They mean that he's on the job.*

('Gob', incidentally, not only meant 'lots' in American slang. It was also the slang for 'sailor'.)

Barnacle Bill the Sailor was a popular character in America. There was a whole series of songs about him that extolled the glories of navy life. In *Here I Go To Tokio*, Barnacle Bill describes vital preliminary action before he whips Hirohito, 'the dirty little so-and-so', on his way to Tokyo.

> *They gave me leave to come ashore,*
> *To see a gal I had before,*
> *And here I am right at her door,*
> *Said Barnacle Bill the Sailor.*

The years following the First World War had produced an explosion in dancing as a form of popular entertainment. Hundreds of dance halls and ballrooms dotted the land, some attracting a thousand or more patrons each night. They were served by literally thousands of dance bands. Some were small ensemble groups; others were full orchestras. Their

quality varied enormously, and many faded into obscurity. But the most famous of these bands (those led by Ambrose, Geraldo, Jack Hylton, Jack Payne, Lew Stone) were among the best in the world and seriously rivalled anything – Armstrong, Ellington, Goodman, even the great Glenn Miller himself – that America had to offer. The declaration of war changed all that.

Conscription wreaked havoc with the big bands of the day. Most of the bandleaders were too old to be called up, but there were some exceptions. One notable bandleader who was called up was Sidney Lipton. He was commissioned as an officer in the Royal Signal Corps in 1941, and served throughout the war, leading a first-class army dance orchestra. However, younger musicians had no immunity from conscription and were called up in their thousands. But popular music didn't suffer, as the bands' loss was the services' gain: so many top musicians were now in the armed forces that each branch of the service was able to form its own top-class dance band. The navy had its swing octet the Blue Mariners, while the army fielded the Royal Army Ordnance Corps Blue Rockets. Even the marines had their own dance band – the Royal Marine Commando Training Orchestra (better known as the Marineers). But the best bands of all were those of the RAF.

Realizing the importance of music for morale purposes the RAF's Director of Music, Wing Commander R.P. O'Donnell (brother of B. Walton O'Donnell, conductor of the BBC Military Band) let it be known that he was recruiting members for new bands. These were to be a new sort of military band that would be used to entertain at RAF bases. Unlike those of previous wars, they would not be for marching or close-order drill (never a high priority in the RAF in any event, and largely redundant in the

JACK HYLTON (IN SUIT) WITH HIS PRE-WAR BAND BEFORE HE BECAME A LEADING IMPRESSARIO.

mechanized warfare to come), but rather to provide popular entertainment for military personnel. His call was answered by musicians up and down the country, who all beat a path to the RAF camp in Uxbridge. Because of O'Donnell's imaginative planning there can be no doubt that the RAF had the cream of the conscripted swing and jazz musicians, and their Squadronaires and Skyrockets were regarded as the best bands in uniform. Four members of Ambrose's famous orchestra, all eligible for call-up, immediately volunteered for the RAF. They were soon joined by other ex-Ambrose players and became the core of what was to become the most famous British swing band of the war, the No. 1 RAF Dance Orchestra, more popularly known as the Squadronaires or, to its many admirers, simply the Squads. It was initially led by Sgt Leslie Holmes (stage name, Les Brannelly) and, later, by Sgt Jimmy Miller, a former vocalist and guitarist with Ambrose. The Squadronaires also had among their personnel some of the finest British 'sidemen' of all time, including drummer Jock Cummings, trumpet players Tommy McQuater and Kenny Baker and, of course, Cliff Townsend (father of Who star, Peter). Baker was given the supreme accolade as 'the musicians' musician', and is probably Britain's greatest ever 'man with a golden horn'. (He is, at the time of writing, still active and playing.)

The chief function of these new-style military bands was to provide entertainment for the troops. Primarily, this was dance music in service entertainment centres and clubs. After D-Day the bands continued their entertainment at military recreation centres on the Continent. The very best also appeared on radio broadcasts and made records. These bands helped keep up the spirits of millions of soldiers and civilians, providing them with a touch of their home atmosphere, even when they were far from home.

But although it was clear that hundreds of musicians, both classical and dance band, had joined the armed services to do their duty for King and country in whatever form that might take, the dance-band world as a whole did not escape the fifth columnist, shirker and 'lead swinger' accusations that were rife. The *Daily Express*, in an article in its issue of 26 June 1941, stated that 'Many dance band boys dodge the Army!' There was simply no evidence whatsoever to support this accusation, as *Melody Maker* was quick to point out in its vitriolic response to the attack.

The finger of suspicion was pointed even more forcefully at many musicians who were not actively serving in the forces, especially if they had a foreign-sounding name. There was a very strong rumour in circulation that top pianist Charlie Kunz had been arrested for sending messages to the Germans via his piano-playing during his many broadcasts for BBC Radio, and that he was subsequently

imprisoned in the Tower of London for a sentence estimated at between seven and twenty years. It must have been a surprise, to say the least, to those who believed this nonsense to listen to the broadcasts Charlie Kunz continued to make throughout the war. Perhaps they thought he had a piano in his cell in the Tower.

Another rumour concerned French bandleader Ray Ventura, uncle of the internationally known nightclub entertainer Sacha Distel. The story, instigated by Italian propaganda, was that Ventura had been killed fighting for the Finns against the Russians. Again, the British press was quick to pick up on this whispered gossip – little has changed over the years! – and they began to give the 'charge' credibility under such headlines as 'A Dance Band Quisling'. For many years after the war, Ventura, like his fellow Frenchman the film star Maurice Chevalier, found it very difficult to live down the accusation that he had collaborated with the Germans.

For more than just musicians, however, the call to arms occasioned by the declaration of war resulted in a massive call-up of men. For most of them the army was a new and alien experience. One way they found to deal with the rude shock of army life was through song. *Kiss Me Goodnight, Sergeant Major* mocked the lack of domestic comforts and homely, tender loving care to be found in the army. This song, by Art Noel and Don Pelosi, still has that strong 'chuckle factor' fifty years on:

> *Kiss me goodnight, Sergeant Major,*
> *Tuck me in my little wooden bed.*
> *We all love you, Sergeant Major,*
> *When we hear you bawling 'Show a leg'.*
> *Don't forget to wake me in the morning,*
> *And bring me round a nice cup of tea.*
> *Kiss me goodnight, Sergeant Major,*
> *Sergeant Major be a mother to me.*

Another favourite with the recruits was Jimmy Hughes and Frank Lake's *Bless 'Em All*. This widely sung song was the enlisted men's anthem. In highly regimented army life, it was one of the few acceptable ways of having a dig at one's officers. The rousing lyric that has come down to us through wartime recordings catches the gusto with which the song was sung, but is perhaps not the soldiers' most popular rendition of it. Away from the recording devices – in billets, on troopships, in pubs – a verb far ruder than any to pass the lips of Gracie Fields (the song's most popular exponent) was used.

> *There's many an airman has blighted*
>   *his life*
> *Thru' writing rude words on the wall.*
> *You'll get no promotion this side of*
>   *the ocean,*
> *So cheer up, my lads, bless 'em all.*

But for sheer inventiveness, the prize must surely go to the marathon lyric of *In the Quartermaster's Stores*. This song, by Elton Box, Desmond Cox and Bert Reed (and countless squaddies who added their own verses), poked fun at the quality of

life in the army. A singalong song with limitless verses, it was popular in barrack-rooms in every theatre of war and never failed to rouse its audience. The lyrics included references to all the pet gripes that bedevilled the squaddies: 'bread like lumps of lead', buns that were like 'bullets for the guns, mice 'eating up the rice', rats 'as big as bloomin' cats', 'meat you couldn't eat', eggs 'nearly growing legs', beer 'you can't get near', 'rum for the General's tum', 'cake you couldn't break', flies 'feeding on the pies' and many, many more verses that became progressively more unsavoury with every new rhyme.

Songs such as *In the Quartermaster's Stores* and *Oh How I Hate to Get Up in the Morning* were greatly appreciated by the new recruits to the armed forces. Most of these young men had never been away from home before, so songs such as these helped them to cope with the unexpected rigours of military life. Not only did they help the soldiers laugh at the discomforts they had to experience, but they also helped to show that the men were not alone in their discomfort.

Once the war had started, such was the determination to destroy Hitler and his Nazi regime that Britain quickly moved into top gear. Only a month after the declaration of war, British troops were already in Europe. In October 1939 the British Expeditionary Force crossed the Channel to link up with the Allied line in Lille. This marked the first of the many mass movements of soldiers and civilians that were to characterize the next six years. It also saw the first of the countless thousands of dockside and railway-station farewells and reunions that continued without respite for the entire war.

Songwriters rose to the occasion with some of their best efforts to mirror these scenes. *We'll Meet Again* was one of the most poignant of all songs of separation. It was written by one of Britain's most successful and prolific songwriting teams, Ross Parker and Hughie Charles (who also scored a great success with *There'll Always be an England*). During the course of the war, the song was sung by literally thousands of performers, and recorded in dozens of cover versions, but (along with that other favourite, *The White Cliffs of Dover*) it will always be associated with British 'Forces Sweetheart' Vera Lynn. *We'll Meet Again* encapsulated the feelings of the wartime generation, filling millions of couples with the hope that some day their separation would end, that they'd have their longed-for safe reunion 'some sunny day'.

We'll meet again, don't know where,
don't know when,

This is the army

IRVING BERLIN ON STAGE DURING A TOURING PERFORMANCE OF 'THIS IS THE ARMY'.

Songs that celebrated army life reached their peak with Irving Berlin's theatrical show 'This is the Army'. Already fifty-three years old by the time America entered the war (and having already served in the First World War), Berlin was considered too old to be allowed to enlist again. Instead, he turned his formidable energy to producing the mammoth flag-waving revue. The show was enormously popular: stage versions toured in both America and Britain. Additionally Berlin himself took it (and the 300 soldier cast) on the road to tour military camps in all theatres of war.

The revue provided a mildly satirical view of army life. One of the most popular songs in the show was the number *Oh! How I Hate to Get Up in the Morning* sung by Berlin himself in a facsimile of his First World War uniform (which was highly appropriate in the circumstances as Berlin, famed in the music industry for his acumen, recycled the song from his First World War musical, 'Yip Yip Yaphank'). The lyrics of such songs as *This is the Army Mr Jones* and *Oh! How I Hate to Get Up in the Morning* captured with wit and good humour the changed circumstances with which the new recruit was confronted.

> *This is the army Mr Jones,*
> *No private rooms or telephones.*
> *You've had your breakfast in bed before,*
> *But you won't get it here any more.*

They helped smooth the transition from civilian to soldier and were enjoyed by servicemen everywhere. The 1943 film version (in which Berlin sang *Oh! How I Hate to Get Up in the Morning*) helped the show reach an even larger audience.

> *But I know we'll meet again some*
> *   sunny day.*
> *Keep smilin' thru' just like you*
> *   always do,*
> *Till the blue skies drive the dark*
> *   clouds far away.*

The trauma of wartime separation and departure generated other powerful songs as well. Some have since faded into obscurity, others have had their meanings changed by subsequent events, but they all had particular resonances for the couples torn apart by the war. Two of the best were Michael Carr's *Somewhere in France With You* and Roy King and Stanley Hill's *I'll Pray for You*.

Somewhere in France With You is the lament of a girl back home whose thoughts are always with her loved one stationed overseas in France. At a time when the only activity of British soldiers

You Must Remember This...

overseas was seemingly meaningless sentry duty, such separations were particularly hard to bear. Later, after the British retreat at Dunkirk and the fall of France, the song took on a new meaning.

I'll Pray for You was an expression of the simultaneous fear and hope that were constantly with those parted by the war.

> *I'll pray for you*
> *While you're away.*
> *Each night and day*
> *I'll pray for you,*
> *Till troubles cease.*
> *Then you and I*
> *Will live in peace.*
> *Tho' my tears are falling,*
> *A smile will still remain,*
> *The smile that I'll be saving,*
> *To greet you back again.*
> *My love for you will brightly burn*
> *Till you return.*
> *I'll pray for you,*
> *I'll pray for you.*

Not all songs were expressions of longing. As the boys went off to war, they sang their own favourite morale-boosters. One with an unlikely origin was *South of the Border*. Although songs about distant, exotic places were popular throughout the war – not least because they provoked images of exotic fantasy far removed from the grim reality – *South of the Border* was a particular favourite with the troops. Although the song is most often associated

'FORCES SWEETHEART' VERA LYNN AT THE OPENING OF THE YMCA MOBILE CANTEEN, A GIFT TO THE FORCES FROM THE VARIETY ARTISTES LADIES GUILD.

with American cowboy singer Gene Autry, it was actually written by the leading British songwriting team of Jimmy Kennedy and Michael Carr. In an astute wartime move, the music's publisher took the picture of an alluring Mexican señorita off the cover and replaced her with a squad of Scotties. A new subtitle for the song – 'The Tommies' Theme Song' – completed its transformation and it quickly became one of the most popular of the war years.

Kennedy and Carr joined forces to create another great favourite of the squaddies, *We're Gonna Hang Out the Washing on the Siegfried Line*. This song was written in innocence of the true horrors that lay ahead and its suggestion

DAILY EXPRESS, 7 SEPTEMBER 1939.

that the war would be quickly concluded made it doubly attractive to many listeners. It is written in a style more reminiscent of the First World War which, owing to its origins, is not, perhaps, surprising. The song was inspired by a cartoon in the *Daily Express*. Hoping to repeat the success of the 'Old Bill' cartoon character from the First World War, the *Daily Express*'s brilliant cartoonist, Bobbie St John Cooper, created a new character more in tune with contemporary events. The cartoon featured as its main character 'Young Bert', who was posted, in the popular phrase of the time, 'somewhere in France'. In one panel Young Bert wrote home to his mother to say that he was sending home a length of Hitler's Siegfried Line for her to hang her washing on. Kennedy and Carr immediately saw the line's potential and created one of the most enduring songs of the Second World War.

We're Gonna Hang Out the Washing on the Seigfried Line was the outstanding songwriting success of the Phoney War period. But the same cheeky impudence

WHILE SOME DANCE, OTHERS STUDY THE GIANT SONG-SHEET OF ONE OF THE WAR'S MOST POPULAR SONGS, *WE'RE GONNA HANG OUT THE WASHING ON THE SIEGFRIED LINE.*

that endeared the song to the British public struck a different note with the Germans. With its bragging contempt for their defensive masterpiece, that massive chain of fortifications they called their West Wall, *We're Gonna Hang Out the Washing on the Siegfried Line* was one of the few songs produced during the war that actually infuriated the Nazi leaders. During the Occupation of Europe, German military bands played the song in derision and to show contempt for Britain. After the expulsion of the Germans the tables were turned once again as the citizens of Brussels and other formerly occupied capitals welcomed their liberators with, you guessed it, *We're Gonna Hang Out the Washing on the Siegfried Line*.

Although *We're Gonna Hang Out the Washing on the Siegfried Line* is, arguably, the most popular song of the Second World War, it was in fact banned by some American radio stations, for fear of infringing their country's neutrality. It was not until the United States had entered the war, in December 1941, that such songs were broadcast in America. Even then, *We're Gonna Hang Out the Washing on the Siegfried Line* never gained the popularity in the United States that it had in Britain. In the release of their pent-up emotions, the American song-writers pandered to baser instincts in such compositions as *Bye, Bye Benito*, *He'll Put an Ax to the Axis*, *We're Going to Find a Fellow Who is Yellow and Beat Him Red,* *White and Blue,* and *We're Gonna Have to Slap That Dirty Little Jap*. Songs such as these were part of the rush of jingoistic songs popular at the time of the declaration of war both in Britain and later in the USA.

The cockiness expressed before D-Day in Sgt Joe Bushkin and Pvt John De Vries's *There'll be a Hot Time in the Town of Berlin (When the Yanks Go Marching In)* is typical of such songs. *There'll be a Hot Time in the Town of Berlin* was a great favourite of the American troops and the snappy song was covered by many leading artists of the day. With a lyric that said

> *We're gonna take a hike*
> *Through Hitler's Reich,*
> *And change 'Heil' to 'Whatcha*
>   *know Joe'.*

they made clear their commitment to finish the job.

A much truer reflection of events that were taking place could be seen in the dance halls up and down the British Isles. It was there that the real mood of the nation was captured in the music it danced to, and the songs it sang. Unsurprisingly, almost half of the hit titles of the period had a wartime theme. None, however, was more stirring than a singalong song written by the ubiquitous Ross Parker and Hugh Charles. Their *There'll Always be an England* became the nation's rallying cry, uniting Britons as one in the fight against the Reich. So popular was the song that it came to be regarded as the second national anthem.

There'll Always be an England was written on the eve of fighting in order to, in the words of Hughie Charles, 'counter-act despair' in the inevitable lurch towards war in 1939. It was premiered in the film 'Discoveries' based on Carroll Levis's popular radio show. The song, sung by Master Glyn Davies, the Welsh boy soprano, was hastily tacked on as a grand finale of almost Busby Berkeley-like proportions in which Davies was dressed in a snappy midshipman's uniform surrounded by a huge chorus of bell-bottomed sailors. Such was its popularity that it went straight to the top of the bestseller list. Within two months of the declaration of war, 200,000 copies of the sheet music had been sold. Today, its echoes of an all-conquering England and its imperialistic overtones may fall beyond the bounds not only of political correctness but also of taste — and, unlike other songs with a similar message, *Rule Britannia* and *Land of Hope and Glory*, it has faded from popularity — but during the war there was no better patriotic call to arms.

> *There'll always be an England, while*
> *   there's a country lane,*
> *Wherever there's a cottage small, beside a*
> *   field of grain.*
> *There'll always be an England, while*
> *   there's a busy street,*
> *Wherever there's a turning wheel,*
> *   a million marching feet.*

> *Red, white and blue,*
> *What does it mean to you?*
> *Surely you're proud,*
> *Shout it aloud.*
> *Britons awake,*
> *The Empire too,*
> *We can depend on you.*
> *Freedom remains.*
> *These are the chains nothing can break.*
> *There'll always be an England,*
> *   and England shall be free,*
> *If England means*
> *   as much to you*
> *As England*
> *   means to me.*

As this aptly demonstrates, the songs of the Second World War provided a well-needed optimism. All over Europe the Allies were folding as the Nazis conquered and crushed country after country: Czechoslovakia, Poland, Denmark, Norway, Holland — all were soon under the heel of the German jackboot, with the final humiliation of the conquest of France looming on the horizon.

CHAPTER THREE

The Phoney War

Everybody Do the Blackout Stroll

THE DISMEMBERMENT of Czechoslovakia in March 1939 confirmed what many people were dreading: war was inevitable. There were diplomatic attempts to shore up the crumbling policy of appeasement, but also increasing preparations for war. These shifted into top gear in September 1939. With the German invasion of Poland on 1 September the war that everyone dreaded had at last begun. The experience of aerial bombardment in the First World War was now compounded by the terrifying example of the effect of aerial bombing on civilian populations which had already been brought home by the recent events in Guernica during the Spanish Civil War. This resulted in a heightened awareness of the devastation that could be rained down on defenceless cities. One alarming government report estimated that 600,000 civilians would be killed in the first two months of fighting. In the light of

GRIN AND BEAR IT. MOTHERS AND THEIR CHILDREN PREPARE TO LEAVE FOR SAFE AREAS – 28 SEPTEMBER 1940.

such projections, it comes as no surprise that some 3.5 million people left the cities for safer areas.

For the purposes of evacuation planning, the country was divided into three types of areas. The first category – London and the cities – were places reckoned to be at the greatest risk of bombing. These were designated as 'evacuation' areas. That is, they were places from which outward movement was encouraged. The second area category was designated 'neutral'. These were places that had a low risk of bombing but in and out of which movement was prohibited. The third category was 'reception' areas. It was here that the evacuees from category-one areas would be relocated.

The last day of August 1939 saw the voluntary evacuation of schoolchildren from London. 1.3 million children in 4,000 special trains departed for the reception areas from seventy-two London transport stations. Nor was the evacuation limited to the capital. When the blitz began children were evacuated from coastal cities – Hull, Chatham, Portsmouth, Rochester – as well.

Before the war's end there would be some 60 million changes of address in England and Wales (out of a total civilian population of about 38 million) and countless more among members of the armed forces. By early 1940 – before the blitz began – London had lost over a quarter of its population, Essex 16 per cent, and Kent 11 per cent. At the same time the population of the reception areas soared: the figures in Buckinghamshire and Berkshire increased by more than a third and in Cornwall by almost 20 per cent. Scarcely a family in the country remained unaffected by this massive movement of people.

The first wartime evacuations began immediately. Within four days of the declaration of war over a million schoolchildren and nearly half a million mothers with children under the age of five had been moved from their homes in the cities to the safer reception areas. Yet this first evacuation was for many people short-lived. When the government's dire predictions failed to materialize and the bombs failed to fall, many people drifted back to the still unbombed cities. By Christmas, half of the evacuated school-children and almost 90 per cent of the mothers with young children had returned to the cities. Little could they have realized that a second wave of evacuations was just around the corner.

The separation of millions of mothers and fathers from their children produced the first really popular song of

the Phoney War, the tear-jerking *Goodnight Children, Everywhere*. Although today the words seem excessively sentimental, they profoundly moved people whose families had been so suddenly wrenched apart. The song was popularized by Gracie Fields, who sang it not only for audiences in Britain, but also included it in her ENSA Christmas concerts for the British Expeditionary Force (BEF) in France.

The song's dedication, 'With a tender thought to all evacuated children', had a particular resonance for the mothers of the children who were evacuated in the early days of the war. The song's title was also heavy with meaning. It came from the closing message used by the anchor figure Derek 'Uncle Mac' McCullough at the end of his highly popular BBC Home Service radio programme for young listeners, 'The Children's Hour'. 'Uncle Mac' used to end each programme with the sign-off phrase, 'Goodnight children, everywhere.' And if his trademark pause between the words 'children' and 'everywhere' did not set lips trembling, then Gracie Fields' song, with its lines 'Your mummy thinks of you tonight' and 'Though you are far away, she's with you night and day', never failed to do so.

Goodnight children, everywhere,
Your mummy thinks of you tonight.
Lay your head on your pillow,
Don't be a kid or a weeping willow

Gracie – who had already found international fame and fortune with such comic songs as *The Biggest Aspidistra in the World, He's Dead But He Won't Lie Down* and *Out in the Cold, Cold Snow* – later recorded another wet-handkerchief lullaby which became a smash hit – *I'm Sending a Letter to Santa Claus (To Bring Daddy Safely Home to Me)*.

Tugging almost as hard, albeit at rather different emotions, was *My Heart Belongs to Daddy*.

If I invite a boy some night,
To dine on my fine fin and haddy,
It may be true
I might follow through,
But my heart belongs to Daddy.

It was originally sung by sultry Pat Kirkwood in the November 1939 hit West End show 'Black Velvet'. And while it was definately not *paternal* feelings that it stirred, nevertheless, like *Goodnight Children, Everywhere*, it was perfectly timed to appeal to servicemen stationed in Europe over Christmas, for no apparent purpose, in the Phoney War.

The evacuation was not restricted to people. Many institutions also left the cities. Schools, hospitals, government departments – all moved to safer areas. The BBC, for example, moved to Bristol and, later, when the Bristol docks came under attack, to Evesham and Bedford. Even the famed Billingsgate fish market moved – to Maidstone. But it was the coastal towns of the southeast (where

(BELOW): 'BIG-HEARTED' ARTHUR ASKEY
PREPARES TO DO BATTLE WITH A SAND BAG.
(RIGHT): LINE ENGAGED AT THE TELEPHONE
EXCHANGE AS OPERATORS PRACTISE GASMASK
DRILL.

invasion was expected) that suffered most from evacuation. Many were almost completely depopulated. Folkestone, for example, saw its population drop from 46,000 to just 6,000.

Of course, preparation for the impending war was not limited to the movement of civilians to safer areas. As Britain moved on to a war footing buildings were sandbagged to protect them from blast damage, trenches were dug in parks and streets to provide temporary shelter (making night-time traverses of London's parks particularly hazardous for courting couples), and gasmasks were distributed.

The materials for making back-garden Anderson shelters (earth-covered metal sheeting named after Sir John Anderson, later Minister of Home Security) were also supplied. As was the case with gasmasks, the distribution of the Anderson shelters began months before the declaration of war. They were positive proof – if any were needed – of the government's conviction that the coming war was not only inevitable but would be on a scale previously unknown to Britain.

It was at this time that the fierce ARP (Air Raid Precautions) wardens entered the public consciousness. Many veterans of the First World War, too old to enlist again, looked for other ways to serve the country. Some became wardens

in the ARP. Although it was not until some time later that they were properly kitted out in the official blue overalls that became their uniform, they took to their task with relish. Initially equipped with little more than a steel helmet, a bell to warn of bombs and a wooden rattle to warn of gas attacks, the ARP wardens conscientiously patrolled their patches, ensuring that blackout precautions were adhered to strictly and that gasmasks were always to hand.

ARP wardens (men and women) were often the butt of humour, but they played an essential role, not least in the raising of war consciousness. Their duties were varied and although they bore no arms they were, in a real sense, Britain's first line of defence. They were the first to arrive at an incident – be it a fire or UXB (unexploded bomb) – and they were crucial in routeing information to the central Civil Defence Control Posts, which then coordinated a prompt and appropriate response to the situation. The wardens also put out minor fires, gave first aid, and directed people to shelters at the start of an air raid.

Many of the ARP wardens had first-hand experience of the horrific effects of mustard gas and other chemical weapons from the First World War. This may have contributed to the seriousness with which they approached their new responsibilities. But it was hard for the general public to take seriously the ridiculous-looking 'respirators' that they were forced to carry with them at all times. As George Formby sang in *I Did What I Could with Me Gas Mask.*

> *Now I'm getting very fond of me*
>   *gasmask, I declare.*
> *It hardly ever leaves my side.*
> *I sling it on me back,*
> *And I take it everywhere.*

Mister Brown of London Town looked at the contribution of civilian ARP wardens rather more soberly. The song came from Emile Littler's show 'More 1066' although it gained even greater popularity when played in the dance halls (as it was a song to which one could do the Lambeth Walk). The song was about an ARP warden, the eponymous Mr Brown, and his commitment to duty.

> *Mister Brown of London town*
> *Had a job to do.*
> *Meant to see it through,*
> *And he did it, too.*
> *Mister Brown of London town*
> *Sent the wife away,*

The Phoney War

Sent the kids to play,
Miles and miles away.
Things blew up and things blew down,
Seemed a blinkin' shame.
Bloomin' fire and flame,
Blimey what a game!
But who stood up and saved
*   the town,*
When London Bridge was falling
*   down?*
Mister Brown of London town.

But the job most people remember the ARP wardens was their stringent enforcement of blackout regulations. This duty, onerous but essential, often earned wardens the nickname of 'Little Hitler' for their reports of such minor infringements as lighting cigarettes in the street (in the fear that they would be visible to enemy pilots). The courts were clogged with cases such as these brought by over-zealous ARP wardens, and their shouted command, 'Put that light out!', itself became something of a joke. Another politically incorrect song of wartime, this time sung by George Formby, poked fun at a Chinese laundryman-cum-air raid warden, the eponymous Mr Wu.

He goes around every night
To make the blackout sure.
So if you've got a chink in your window,
Hey, you'll have another one at your door.

The blackout generated its own songs. *Everybody Do the Blackout Stroll* and *Crash! Bang! I Want to Go Home* were just two of

A LIFE-SIZED DUMMY, 'AIR RAID ARCHIE', PROVED TO BE THE MOST SUCCESSFUL RECRUITING OFFICER IN MALDEN AND COOMBE IN MAY 1938.

the many songs that made light of the blackout. Even existing songs were modified to take account of the blackout. For example, a topical verse quickly added to the already popular *Lambeth Walk* went:

Down the inky avenue,
Inky, pinky, parlez-vous,
You'll find your way,
Doing the Lambeth Walk, Oi!

Everybody do the Blackout Stroll contained the immortal line 'Laugh and drive your cares right up the pole' – unfortunately, it wasn't only cares that were driven up the pole. There was a massive increase in traffic accidents when the blackout regulations first came into force. In London, road accidents trebled as drivers continued to

negotiate blacked-out streets with blacked-out headlights. Such was the carnage on the roads — which almost threatened to exceed that of aerial bombardment — that it forced a slight relaxation in regulations: small slits were thereafter permitted in the shades which masked headlamps. This only slightly alleviated the problem, as drivers continued to career around the darkened streets. It was only once petrol was rationed that a semblance of safety returned to the city.

Nor was it drivers alone who risked their lives moving about in the blacked out streets.

Pedestrians, too, suffered appalling injuries — and not only from cars. Many did themselves serious injury by walking into lamp posts and other

'SHOW ME THE WAY TO GO HOME.' PAINTING WHITE LINES ON ROADS, TREES, AND PILLAR BOXES WAS COMPULSORY DURING THE BLACKOUT.

obstructions. So serious was the problem that the government launched an official campaign to warn people about the hazards of leaping off moving buses (and into pillar boxes and lamp posts) in blackouts. More worryingly, several pedestrians were reported to have fallen into canals and drowned. In *Follow the White Line*, Arthur Riscoe recounted one strategy for dealing with the blackout — and the difficulties experienced by a patron of the Rose and Crown as he tried to make his way home.

Follow the white line all the way...
And no matter where you roam,
It will take you after dark
Round the railings in the park
And back again to home sweet home.

While the enforcement of blackout regulations and the inconvenience it caused was widely resented during the Phoney War, not all people had cause to complain. *They Can't Black Out the Moon* by Art Strauss, Bob Dale and Sonny Miller, showed that even this dark cloud had its silver lining. The song starts with a courting couple exclaiming 'Gee, but it's nice in the dark with the moon and you'. It continues:

When we go strolling in the park at
night,
Oh! the darkness is a boon.
Who cares if we're without light?
They can't black out the moon.

But six years of blackout was testing even

for the most adoring couples. Most people longed for the day when the lights would go back on again. So powerful was this sentiment that its imagery came to symbolize the end of the war in many later songs. But for now, few people disagreed with Helen Thomas's *In London Town at Night*:

Some day there'll be lights in London
town at night,
For the hopes of men are burning strong
and bright;
London folks will carry on to a
new and glorious dawn,
And the lights will shine in
London town at night.

As well as organizing large-scale evacuations and imposing air-raid drills and blackout regulations, the government made panicky decisions in the field of entertainment. One of the most bitterly resented came at the outbreak of the war when the fear of bombs resulted in a decree that all theatres should be closed. Many London Theatres decamped to rural areas – to the chagrin of Londoners but to the enjoyment of provincial theatre-goers. Only the tiny Windmill in Old Compton Street, Soho, with its 'girlie' revues, defied the ban, boosting the morale of servicemen on leave and displaying the proud boast 'We Never Closed!' above its entrance. So important was the Windmill's contribution to morale-raising

that it became legendary. In the wartime movie 'Tonight and Every Night', actress Rita Hayworth played a chorine from a theatre that could only have been the Windmill. In the film, she turns down a proposal of marriage from her RAF pilot boyfriend so she can carry on with the show – her contribution to the war effort being more important than her own personal happiness. Such is the stuff of myth.

Cinemas, too, came under strict control. Initially they, like theatres, were ordered to close. But soon wiser heads in government realized the importance of the cinema and theatre for morale purposes, and the restrictions were relaxed – although cinemas in areas suffering the effects of the blitz still had a curfew of 6pm. Even in areas considered safe from bombing, cinemas were only permitted to remain open until 10pm – and blackout

WINDMILL GIRLS TAKE A BREAK IN THEIR DRESSING-ROOM IN THE THEATRE THAT NEVER CLOSED.

You Must Remember This...

restrictions could still make the night-time journey home hazardous in the extreme.

The declaration of war on 3 September 1939 brought huge changes to the lives of ordinary people. The cumulative effect of the blackouts, curfews, rationing and restrictions was enormous. Yet by the winter of that year they all seemed to have been in vain. Contrary to predictions by both the government and the more volatile press, the war seemed to many to have fizzled out. Poland had been defeated in a matter of weeks – long before the first members of the BEF landed in France – and since that time German belligerence seemed to have abated. British troops in France grumbled with boredom as the expected attack never came.

The Phoney War grated on the nerves of those serving in the armed forces. Perhaps this helps to account for the fact that few memorable forces songs were written in the period, and, indeed, several have been consigned to the dustbin of songwriting. The senior service was in no mood for *Oh, Ain't it Grand to be in the Navy* after the loss of the aircraft carrier *Courageous* and the battleship *Royal Oak* in quick succession. And *Reckless Jeff of the RAF* won few fans at a time when the air force was doing little more than dropping leaflets on the enemy. Whether it was the desire not to tempt fate or merely memories of broken promises made in the First World War, *We Won't Be Long Out There* never took off. On the other hand, *We're Gonna Hang Out the Washing on the Siegfried Line* still maintained its popularity, even though it, too, was one of the few songs that encouraged a belief that the war might be over quickly. However, after the massive retreat at Dunkirk and the fall of France the song had, for some, rather a hollow ring to it. Nevertheless, according to Winston Churchill's chauffeur, disaster on the Continent notwithstanding, the great man used to hum the refrain in the back of the car on his way to War Cabinet meetings.

The Phoney War

The Phoney War sorely tried the patience of the civilian population. If the summer of 1939 had been one of the most glorious on record, the winter of 1939–40 was one of the most severe. With restrictions on fuel and the nuisance of the seemingly irrelevant blackout beginning to bite, public disaffection grew. The situation got worse in January 1940 when the first of the wartime rationing measures on food were introduced. When the aerial bombardments failed to materialize, many evacuees left the reception areas and returned to the cities. By early 1940 discontent was widespread. The most tangible evidence of the war was increased government bureaucracy (and inefficiency), increased deprivation and the proliferation of apparently meaningless restrictions. (There were 50,000 civil servants in the Ministry of Food alone – all seemingly intent on imposing the misery of rationing). In the face of all these apparently petty restrictions there was still little indication that Britain really was at war. Although there were some naval actions off far-distant shores, these had little impact at home. The sarcastic *I'm One of the Whitehall*

Warriors certainly caught the mood of a disgruntled nation.

> *At a stroke of the pen, I set thousands of men*
> *Making bicycle clips for the troops.*
> *I supply every button and shoulder of mutton*
> *And sample the various soups.*

On 14 May 1940, just days after the German invasion of the Low Countries and France, Anthony Eden, the Secretary of State for War, called for volunteers to

join the newly created Local Defence Volunteers, better known to us as the Home Guard. Within twenty-four hours a quarter of a million men answered his call, and by July they numbered over a million. Although the Home Guard has been the object of a certain amount of derision, it was a heartfelt response to the nation's needs in the face of the expected invasion by those individuals unable to join the regular army because of their age or because they were engaged in essential occupations.

In the George Formby film 'Get Cracking' George joins the Home Guard with predictable results. The title song of the film, *(When the Lads of the Village) Get Crackin'*, written by Formby and Eddie Latta, was one of the first songs to feature the exploits of the Home Guard.

It's the Home Guard going on parade.
Every British son,
Shouldering a gun,
Out to show the stuff from which
they're made.

It was Spike Milligan who noted that 'music was as important as ammunition'. It had to be, for at the outset of hostilities, the country was ill-prepared for war. Unlike Germany, which had been preparing for years – and had even taken the opportunity to try out its weapons and tactics in the bloody Spanish Civil War – Britain had almost nothing with which to fight. The image of the Home Guard as later portrayed by Jimmy Perry and David Croft in the hit BBC situation comedy 'Dad's Army' was uncomfortably close to the truth. The Home Guard,

NOEL COWARD
MAKES HIS OWN CONTRIBUTION
TO THE WAR EFFORT, SINGING HIS OWN BITTINGLY
SATIRICAL *DON'T LET'S BE BEASTLY TO THE GERMANS*.

created on the day Churchill became Prime Minister, was dressed in ill-fitting uniforms (when it had any uniforms at all). The situation with regard to weapons was even more desperate. Sometimes whole units had to share a single rifle – and even that might date back to the Boer War. A First World War Enfield 303 rifle was a prize.

Britain, at last girding its loins, was prepared to follow the Prime Minister's call to 'fight them on the beaches and on the landing grounds, and in the fields and in the streets'. But with what? With devastating wit, Nöel Coward summed up the situation splendidly in his ironic appeal to the Ministry of Defence.

> *Could you please oblige us with a*
> *Bren gun,*
> *Or, failing that, a hand grenade*
> *would do.*
> *We've got some ammunition,*
> *In a rather damp condition,*
> *And Mayor Huss*
> *Has an arquebus*
> *That was used in Waterloo.*
> *With the vicar's stirrup pump,*
> *a pitchfork and a spade,*
> *It's rather hard to guard an aerodrome.*
> *So if you can't oblige us with a Bren gun,*
> *The Home Guard might as well go home.*

CHAPTER FOUR

Defeat on all Fronts

Somewhere in France with You

THE GERMAN INVASION of Denmark and Norway in April 1940, followed quickly by that of the Low Countries and France, brought the uncertainty of the Phoney War to an abrupt end. The Bore War was over. The *blitzkrieg* (literally 'lightning war') tactics employed by the Germans enabled them to overwhelm the meagre resistance these countries were able to offer. One success followed

ALL BEHIND YOU, WINSTON

EVENING STANDARD, **14 MAY 1940.**

another as the Germans blazed forward. On 10 May they swept into the Low Countries and France. In Britain a vote of no confidence forced the discredited Neville ('peace in our

(LEFT): SERGEANT GEORGE MELACHRINO WITH A COMBINED SERVICES ORCHESTRA BROADCASTING TO SERVICE PERSONNEL OVERSEAS.

(ABOVE): Basil Dean, ENSA Director, outside the ENSA HQ at the Drury Lane Theatre.
(RIGHT): Wish us luck as you wave us goodbye. ENSA girls and guy set off to bring a song and a smile to the boys overseas.

time') Chamberlain to resign as Prime Minister and on 10 May Churchill began his own 'finest hour'.

Attempting to rally the stunned nation (and the BEF, reeling under the German assault), Churchill made one of his most famous speeches. However, to his now immortalized words 'I have nothing to offer but blood, toil, tears and sweat' he might also have added ' … and ENSA.' This organization of the nation's entertainers played a vital role in keeping morale high, both for the soldiers in distant outposts in the far-flung theatres of war and on the Home Front. With its stars and lesser-known performers it turned out to be one of Britain's most potent 'secret weapons'. These entertainers gave their services freely, sometimes at great personal risk, in the ENSA cause.

Although dubbed by the more cynical audiences as 'Every Night Something Awful', ENSA was, in fact, one of the most beloved creations of the Second World War. The acronym actually stood for 'Entertainments National Service Association'. The organization was the brainchild of impresario Basil Dean who 'had done something similar' in the First World War. From its headquarters at London's Drury Lane Theatre troupes of entertainers were sent to entertain servicemen all over the world.

ENSA's policy of deploying any willing entertainer – from top professional to rank amateur – could, occasionally, have an adverse effect on the quality of the performances. But this never inter-

fered with ENSA's prime purpose of bringing entertainment and a little bit of home to soldiers in the field.

Fast off the mark, ENSA fielded its first troupes exactly one week after the declaration of war. Their first concert took place at the Old Dene Camp, Camberley, in England, and starred Frances Day and Arthur Riscoe. It took slightly longer for ENSA to get performers overseas. A general reticence in the top brass meant that Dean had to exercise all his powers of persuasion before he finally got permission to take entertainers to the troops in France.

ENSA's first overseas concert party for the BEF took place on 12 November 1939 at a site officially identified only as 'somewhere in France'. (This tour actually made two performances at what we now know were Douai and Arras.) Gracie Fields, who was recovering from a serious operation, left her sickbed to top the bill. Claire Luce and Dennis Noble appeared with her, along with Duveen, the conjuror, and the tap-dancing Three Astors.

After Gracie blazed the trail, many other top artists went to France to entertain the troops. By Christmas 1939 the operation had reached such a scale that even some of the top big bands – Ambrose, Billy Cotton, Joe Loss, Jack Hylton, Jack Payne – made it over. However, had there been a prize awarded to the bandleader who travelled the greatest distance to France in ENSA's cause, it would have surely been won by Carroll Gibbons. American-born bandleader Gibbons had been on holiday in the USA when war was declared. He had to fight a one-man battle with the American authorities in order to return to his home in Britain. Once back, he immediately answered the ENSA call and took his band to France.

The selflessness of these entertainers was greatly appreciated by the troops. They filled a vital role, helping to keep the soldiers' spirits up at a time of crushing boredom and inactivity. ENSA's signature tune, *Let The People Sing*, was a clarion

FLORENCE DESMOND, THE FIRST BRITISH WOMAN ENTERTAINER TO ENTER LIBERATED BRUSSELS, CHOOSES A GLAM FROCK FOR HER NEXT SHOW.

44

VERA LYNN ARRIVING BY RICKSHAW AT THE ENSA THEATRE IN CALCUTTA, IN MAY 1944.

call of normality – and a vital bit of home – that helped dispel the feelings of futility that characterized the Phoney War.

Realizing the benefit that ENSA brought to its audiences, Basil Dean sought to expand its area of influence. Rather than perform just for soldiers, Dean wanted to take ENSA performers to other war workers. Supported by Ernest Bevin, Minister of Labour, the first concert for civilian war workers was held at the Woolwich Arsenal on 22 July 1940.

ENSA gave over 2.5 million entertainments of all kinds during the course of the war. These ranged from grand theatrical performances by top recording artistes to solo performances by unknown singers in the open air. It also ran film and variety shows. All forms of entertainment fell within ENSA's remit –

from opera singers to novelty dancers, from classical musicians to jugglers and comedians. As its head, Basil Dean, recalled: 'The ENSA badge was everywhere.' From the desert tracks of Libya to the jungle tracks of Burma, in Normandy, Italy and, eventually, even in Germany – in every theatre of wartime operation – ENSA troupes followed close behind the combat troops.

George Formby was a mainstay of ENSA throughout the war, entertaining troops in Europe as well as crowds in the shelters at home. Research by the Mass Observation Organization, founded by sociologists Tom Harrison and Charles Madge, confirmed that George Formby was the greatest single morale-booster of them all throughout the entire war. In this he was ahead of the generally accepted 'tie' between Tommy Handley's number one radio show 'ITMA' ('It's That Man Again'), and Winston Churchill.

Formby's immense contribution was officially acknowledged later, on his return from entertaining the troops in the Middle East in June 1944. He was given the ultimate accolade by being invited to take over (from Ed Murrow and J.B. Priestley) the broadcasting of one of their much-listened-to Sunday evening 'Postscripts' radio programmes. Although he never failed to get standing ovations

You Must Remember This...

George Formby could be singing 'Imagine Me on the Piccadilly Line' as he entertains shelterers in the Aldwych Deep Tube Shelter.

wherever he played, Formby modestly stated that his own performances were 'unimportant'. He said that the show really started after he put his ukelele back in its case! The squaddies 'wanted to talk with somebody from home. We used to sit around with mugs of tea – always tea – like a lot of old women gaffing; always about home: What was the beer like? Was it getting stronger? How often does it rain? How is the food – and cigarettes? Are the people being looked after? They were worrying quite a lot about you folks at home, but we soon put them right about that, Beryl [Formby's wife and manager] and I. We told them that after four and a half years at war, Britain was still the best country to live in.'

Some of George's greatest wartime hits were geared especially to the troops. *He Does Look a Swank Does Frank in His Tank, Cookhouse Serenade, Guarding the Home of the Home Guard*, and, of course, his most famous wartime song, *Imagine Me on the Maginot Line*.

> *Hitler can't kid us a lot;*
> *His secret weapon's Tommy rot;*
> *You ought to see the one the*
>   *Sergeant's got*
> *Down on the Maginot Line.*

Perhaps the best proof of the entertainer's enduring qualities is the fact that, fifty years on, his songs are still being sung by the very active George Formby Appreciation Society, who have ukelele-strumming members as young as ten years old, and a quarterly fan club magazine called *The Vellum*.

If there was any entertainer who could compete with George Formby for both the adulation and affection of the

British public, it was Gracie Fields. She, like George, was born in Lancashire and had the same 'I'm just like you lads and lassies out there' rapport with her audiences that he did. Gracie was asked by Basil Dean to be his first major star to entertain the British Forces in France. Although just out of hospital after an operation, Gracie gladly accepted. Together with her husband, Italian-born film director Monty Banks (who made many successful British comedy features), she set sail on her mission to 'cheer up the chaps'. Gracie appeared on makeshift stages, often to the accompaniment of out-of-tune pianos, but it didn't matter – the homesick lads loved her. She sang all her best-known comic numbers and also the wistful ones that reminded them of their beloved Britain which, to many boys of barely eighteen, seemed so far away. Her most requested songs were *Wish Me Luck as You Wave Me Goodbye* and her signature tune *Sally* (the first came from the film 'Shipyard Sally', directed by Monty Banks, the second from 'Sally in Our Alley', which was directed by none other than Basil Dean). It was half a century later, after singing it when top of the bill at a Command performance, that she suddenly announced from the stage to Queen Elizabeth and Prince Philip, sitting happily in the Royal Box: 'D'you know, I've just realized that for the last fifty years I've been singing a *man's* song!' *Sally* contains the line: 'Marry me, Sally, and happy for ever I'll be'.

A few months later things turned sour for Gracie. After she had finished her tour of France and had returned to England, Italy declared war on the Allies. Not only did Gracie fall from public favour because of her marriage to an Italian, but her husband, Monty Banks, was promptly arrested as an enemy alien. Although she continued to work for the war effort both here and in America, British gratitude was not forthcoming at the time, and it was not until after the war that she regained her previous high standing in the hearts of the public.

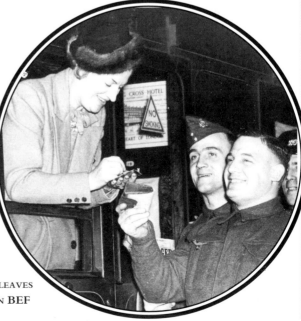

GRACIE FIELDS SIGNS A PARTING AUTOGRAPH AS SHE LEAVES CHARING CROSS STATION ON HER WAY TO ENTERTAIN BEF TROOPS IN FRANCE, IN NOVEMBER 1939.

The comedian 'Big-Hearted' Arthur Askey was another of ENSA's leading lights. He was recruited, as a result of his enormously popular radio show 'Band Waggon', to make some morale-boosting comedy records.

Churchill may have regularly hummed the tune to *We're Gonna Hang Out the Washing on the Siegfried Line*, but he would not have been able to do the same with one of Askey's later excursions into propaganda 'pop' as the chances are he would never have heard it. At the time Askey himself came under what would today be euphemistically called 'friendly fire' for his efforts. It occurred when the comedian recorded *Thanks For Dropping In, Mr Hess*. This ditty was inspired by the mysterious solo flight to Scotland of Germany's Deputy Führer, Rudolph Hess, on 10 May 1941. Apparently Hess had, unbeknownst to Hitler, taken it upon himself to try to negotiate a separate peace with Britain. Hess flew in with his peace terms. After crash-landing his plane in Scotland and breaking his leg he was captured by local farmers. For his pains, Hess never did get his meeting with Churchill and ended up in a series of prisons for the rest of his long life. But if his one-man peace initiative was a failure, it inspired a song whose lyric typified the idiosyncratic, understated, British sense of humour.

Thanks for dropping in, Mr Hess,
We've told your friends to note your new address.
They've heard you've got here safely in Berlin and Rome,
So put way your parachute and make yourself at home.
Thanks for dropping in, Mr Hess.
Forgive the small announcement in the press.
Had you told us you were coming and informed us where you'd land,
We would certainly have had a big reception, nicely planned,
With a carpet and some streamers and

IN A STILL FROM HIS HUGELY SUCCESSFUL SHOW 'BAND WAGGON', ARTHUR ASKEY AND RICHARD 'STINKER' MURDOCH REHEARSE ASKEY'S NEW RECORD, *WE'RE GONNA HANG OUT THE WASHING ON THE SIEGFRIED LINE*.

> *Jack Hylton and his band.*
> *Thanks for dropping in – thanks for*
> *popping in,*
> *What a nice surprise Mr Hess.*

The song was set to a rousing tune, and the records were rushed into the music shops as fast as they came off the press. But almost at once the tens of thousands of 78s were sent back to the issuing record company at double-quick tempo by order of the government. Hypersensitive fainthearts in the government considered it to be 'undiplomatic' to publicize the affair, so the record was withdrawn before it had a single broadcast. Unfortunately for the politicians, however, it was not the end of the story. Askey himself leaked the news to the press which, led by top journalist Hannen Swaffer, really went to town on the absurdity of this government directive. But it was quite some time before the ban was officially lifted and the BBC was finally permitted to play the song.

This incident may well have been in Nöel Coward's mind when his own song *Don't Let's be Beastly to the Germans* was also banned – albeit temporarily – by the government.

> *Don't let's be beastly to the Germans*
> *When victory is ultimately won.*
> *It was just those nasty Nazis who*
> *persuaded them to fight,*
> *And their Beethoven and Bach are really*
> *far worse than their bite.*
> *Let's be meek to them, and turn the other*
> *cheek to them,*
> *And try to bring out their latent sense*
> *of fun.*
> *Let's give them full air parity, and treat the*
> *rats with charity,*
> *But don't let's be beastly to the Hun.*

Although it was one of the few anti-German songs of any artistic merit, and was much appreciated by the more sophisticated (including Churchill, who admired it very much), the song came in for much criticism at the time. Apparently, literal-minded censors could not recognize the subtle irony of the song and so it was initially banned by the BBC. And while the irony restricted the song's more widespread appeal, Coward's wit hit the mark, and time has shown how prophetic he was.

But the euphoria and optimism of the British army in the seven months since they had left the 'white cliffs of Dover' to fight the enemy in the battlefields of Belgium and France were rapidly turning sour. The Allies were giving ground all the time and the casualties were horrendous under continual battering from the German tanks and guns. In every respect, in numbers and equipment, the German military machine was supreme. A period of increasing pessimism culminated in the orders to retreat from Dunkirk, and 'Operation Dynamo', the code name for the evacuation of the British Expeditionary Force, was begun.

The evacuation from Dunkirk was

little less than a miracle. Victory, of a sort, was seized from the jaws of defeat. The armada of 850 boats and ships of all shapes and sizes that answered the call managed to bring back more than 126,000 men from a small strip of Dunkirk Beach during the first four days of the operation. By the completion of the nine-day operation, on 4 June 1940, some 338,226 Allied (mostly British) troops had been evacuated. This heroic feat was treated by the press as 'a victory for freedom'. Halfway around the world the normally sober *New York Times* reported:

> So long as the English tongue survives, the word Dunkirk will be spoken with reverence. For in that harbor, in such a hell as never blazed on earth before, at the end of a lost battle, the rags and blemishes that have hidden the soul of democracy fell away. There, beaten but unconquered, in shining splendour, she faced the enemy.

Many never made it. Some were cut off and were unable to get to the beachhead at Dunkirk, like the 51st Highland Division, who had fought their way to the small fishing village of St Valery-en-Caux, where a memorial to their battle now stands. *The Ballad of St Valery* gives a stark picture that transcends the years of what it must have been like to be there.

The Highland Division, they fought and
they fell,
Although they were battered by shot and
by shell,
Yet they were determined to fight and
go free
Down by St Valery.

That night on the clifftops I'll never
forget,
As we lay on the ground, and it was
soaking wet.
Those memories will ever last for aye
Down by St Valery.

The planes high above us kept dropping
their bombs,
When we on the ground kept singing
our songs.
They thought they had got us, but they
were wrong
Down by St Valery.

Then far out at sea we spied the boys
in blue
Come for to carry us home.

There's a debt that we owe them we can
never repay,
There's a debt we will owe them for many
a day,
And each night in our prayers we will
always say
God bless the boys in blue.

Back in Britain there was jubilation and celebration that the tens of thousands of battle-weary soldiers and sailors were

Defeat on all Fronts

THE MIRACULOUS ESCAPE AT
DUNKIRK – 26 MAY TO 4 JUNE 1940.

home on British shores once more. Then it slowly dawned on the nation that there were no more allies to fight the cause against the seemingly invincible Third Reich. This 'Sceptred Isle' stood alone. This was when Winston Churchill made his most inspiring and unifying speech:

> Let us therefore brace ourselves to do our duty and so bear ourselves that if the British Commonwealth and Empire lasts for a thousand years, men will still say 'This was their finest hour.'

It was at this time that J.B. Priestley, one of Britain's most respected playwrights, began a series of BBC Radio broadcasts entitled 'Postscripts'. On 5 June he stressed the fact that victory was snatched from the jaws of defeat – 'the way in which, when apparently all was lost, so much was gloriously retrieved'. Indeed, with that typically British restrained pro-paganda that emanated from the Central Office of Information, and Churchill's bulldog-breed stance, Dunkirk, far from being a humiliating defeat, had now become in the eyes of the public a tactical conquest. Britain may have been defeated in the battle for France, but it had survived to fight another day.

This posture was ably abetted by the inventive flow of songs that came out of Denmark Street in London's W1, which, because it was the centre of the songwriting industry, was known as Britain's own 'Tin Pan Alley'. It was here that many of the nation's music publishers were located and it was from here that most of the wartime tunes emanated. The products of Denmark Street helped lift the nation from its gloom. It was sing-along and shout defiance time. Several old songs took on new relevance. The last stanza of the favourite *Roll Out the Barrel*, for example, was now sung with extra emphasis.

Careless Talk Costs Lives

This was the time that the Hamburg broadcasts of 'Lord Haw Haw' ('Jairmany calling! Jairmany calling!') were listened to with a mixture of scepticism and uneasiness – 'How does he know that?' – by over half the British public. 'Lord Haw Haw', as he had been scoffingly nicknamed by the British, was later identified as William Joyce, an Irishman born in America, and a one-time member of Sir Oswald Mosley's British Union of Fascists. After the war, Joyce was brought back to England where he was tried for treason. Although he claimed that his place of birth rendered the charge of treason invalid, he was found guilty because he had held a British passport for the first nine months of the war. Joyce was hanged in Wandsworth gaol on 3 January 1946.

One of England's favourite songwriters A.P. Herbert, who had a string of musical credits to his name, did his best to dampen the 'even walls have ears' hysteria that prevailed for a while.

> Do not believe the tale the Milkman tells,
> No troops have mutinied at Potters Bar,
> Nor are there submarines at
>   Tunbridge Wells,
> The BBC will warn us when there are.

The fear of spies and fifth columnists was kept in the public eye by constant exhortations through government information campaigns. In both Britain and America poster campaigns warned that 'You Never Know Who's Listening' (or, as its snappier American version had it, 'Loose Lips Sink Ships'). The sentiment was carried over into popular music. The jaunty *A Slip of the Lip Could Sink a Ship* conveyed a serious message in an accessible way.

> Shh! Don't talk too much.
> Shh! Don't know too much.
> Jack, don't be too hip,
> 'Cause a slip of

the lip might sink a ship.

The importance of the control of information during the war cannot be overestimated. Because of radio, this was the first war in which the public knew about events almost as soon as they happened. Such was the hunger for information that even the acknowledged Nazi propaganda broadcasts of 'Lord Haw Haw' attracted huge audiences. One BBC report stated that two-thirds of the British public listened to him. This was a time when rumour could spread like wildfire and songs like Bill Spillard and John Bach's *Think Twice Before You Speak Once* were intended to counter the rumour-mongering that could disrupt the war effort.

> These are dangerous days we know
>   that's so,
> There's many things the Japs and
>   Hitler want to know.

(*BELOW*): WILLIAM JOYCE (FAR LEFT), THE INFAMOUS TRAITOR 'LORD HAW-HAW', WITH HIS FIRST FASCIST LEADER SIR OSWALD MOSELEY (CENTRE).

Roll out the barrel,
We'll have a barrel of fun.
Roll out the barrel,
We've got the blues on the run.
Sing; boom; Ta-ral-rel,
Ring out a song of good cheer.
Now's the time to roll the barrel
For the gang's all here.

Another big hit of these gloomy days was *You are My Sunshine*. Written by Jimmy Davis and Charlie Mitchell and imported from the USA, its rousing chorus helped lift spirits everywhere.

You are my sunshine,
My only sunshine,
You make me happy,
When skies are grey.

It would be difficult to decide which of these two songs was the most popular of the wartime singalongs. But there was one certainty – during the course of the evening in the dance halls, pubs and clubs, both would be sung with equal gusto.

The loss of France also added a new kind of poignancy to songs previously sung in other contexts. *The Last Time I Saw Paris* and *Somewhere in France with You* became more than simple love songs. They now carried a message of hope, a promise for the future:

There are two blue eyes, such blue eyes
A-smiling at me.
Yet they're lonely as only a woman can be.
For I see all her thoughts are somewhere,
Somewhere in France with you.

VERY WELL, ALONE

Evening Standard, 18 June 1940

The defeat in Europe sobered the nation. The easy optimism of September 1939 was replaced by rapid changes in mood. Now that 'Fortress Britain' awaited the onslaught from air, sea and land, the moods up and down the country swung from the sort of pugnacious defiance displayed by the *Evening Standard*'s cartoonist David Low's soldier – who glared with hostility from a craggy clifftop out towards the shores of France above the caption 'Very Well – Alone' – to the near paranoia about fifth columnists, agents and spies, who were reported to be everywhere.

In these dark hours there wasn't much to cheer about, but Britain found its voice in adversity. Whether by instinct or necessity, the nation had come to realize that laughter is a tonic, and that there was little to equal the power of popular music to raise the spirits.

CHAPTER FIVE

Battle of Britain and the Blitz

The Deepest Shelter in Town

JUST FIVE WEEKS after Dunkirk a new battle began. Reich Marshal Goering's Luftwaffe attempted to sweep the skies clear of all opposition in preparation for Operation Sea Lion, the invasion of Britain. This was Britain's darkest hour and the fate of the nation hung in the balance. After the retreat from Dunkirk, in which most of the BEF's equipment had been abandoned, the only thing that stood in the way of invasion was the RAF. The Battle of Britain was joined.

The situation was at its most critical in August and September 1940. This was a time when a few fighter pilots in the RAF held the fate of the nation in their hands. The odds were stacked heavily against them. Germany had a numerical superiority of

THIS EARLY PROPAGANDA POSTER CAUSED CLASS CONTROVERSY AND WAS QUICKLY WITHDRAWN.

three to one in the air. Yet the nerve of the RAF held and despite being so heavily outnumbered its Spitfires and Hurricanes prevailed. These planes, whose pilots were the glamour boys of the armed services, proved too fast for the Messerschmitts, Heinkels and Junkers. Coastal dog-fights, in which the RAF tenaciously held off the attacking Luftwaffe, became regular aerial spectaculars, with the RAF almost invariably getting the upper hand. The 'first of the few' were, in the words of Michael North and Dave Burnaby, the *Lords of the Air.*

> *England, our island home,*
> *Land of the free.*
> *England, unconquered yet,*
> *O'er land and sea.*
> *Lord of Heavens above,*
> *Answer our prayer.*
> *God keep Britannia's sons,*
> *Lords of the Air,*
> *Lords of the Air!*

The RAF's successes against the Luftwaffe in the Battle of Britain (the Germans lost two planes to every British one shot down) forced a fundamental change in the tactics of aerial warfare. In order to conserve their dwindling air force, the Germans abandoned daylight attacks in favour of safer (for them) night-time bombing. The blitz had begun.

With it, all pretence of bombing only military targets evaporated. As precision bombing was not possible in the dark, the Luftwaffe looked for larger targets. No longer did they attempt to make any distinction between military and civilian targets. With the blitz came a new concept: total war.

From September 1940 through to May 1941, Britain was subjected to almost nightly bombing raids. Contrary to German expectations, however, British morale did not collapse under the onslaught. Indeed, after the initial shock, the nation drew strength from adversity. People took pride in their ability to carry on in the most frightful conditions. The spirit of camaraderie from the shared nightly experience of bombing drew people together. They found, to paraphrase the proverb, that a terror shared was a terror halved.

Music played an important role in helping people deal with their fears. One popular song of the blitz helped them laugh at their own fright at the incessant bombing.

> *Oh what a great big blackout.*
> *How can I make my flat out?*
> *How can I pick my Jack out?*
> *Crash! Bang! I want to go home.*

You Must Remember This...

SPIRITS WERE HIGH EVEN LOW-DOWN IN THE UNDERGROUND.

Don't run away mister,
Oh stay and play mister.
Don't worry if you hear the
sirens go...
...I've got the deepest shelter
in town.

If the social life of the shelters helped to make the air raids bearable, it also generated a new social problem: 'shelter girls'. These were young women who, rather than spending the night at home, went instead to the communal air-raid shelters where they drank and danced the night away – often in the casual company of strangers.

With the coming of the blitz shelter from the air raids assumed a new importance. There were no deep air-raid shelters in London. Although the materials for home-made Anderson shelters had been distributed early in the war, many people preferred the safety (and the relative comfort!) of underground stations to the damp, earth-covered shelters in their own back gardens. Moreover, many preferred the camaraderie of the underground to the loneliness of a night in an Anderson shelter. Florence Desmond, in *The Deepest Shelter in Town*, highlighted some of the advantages of having a deep shelter of one's own.

The breakdown in parental authority caused by the exigencies of the blitz was widely remarked upon at the time. For many young women the blitz provided the perfect excuse to free themselves from the rigid control of their families. For the shelter girls the blitz was liberating.

The blitz was particularly hard on the East End, whose docks made it a prime target. Unfortunately for East Enders, however, there were few back gardens and even fewer underground stations in their part of the city. As a result, many moved into the stations in the centre of the city. Significantly, the government initially resisted the use of

Battle of Britain and the Blitz

underground stations as emergency air-raid shelters on the grounds that it might create a 'shelter psychosis' – a condition at odds with the stiff-upper-lip, Britain-can-take-it stance that was officially encouraged. However, unable to counter the flood of East Enders from the hard-hit docklands, the policy soon changed.

Shared adversity meant that by mid-September 1940 East Enders with their blankets and sandwiches mingled with West Enders with their travelling rugs and picnic hampers in the central London tube stations. True to character, ENSA was quick to respond and on 8 October it provided its first underground concert party with none other than George Formby entertaining the shelterers.

The blitz caused enormous damage. Over 200,000 houses were destroyed and another 1.5 million rendered uninhabitable. Although the numbers killed never reached those forecast by the government in the early days of the war, 20,000 Londoners lost their lives. But, perhaps surprisingly, according to a Mass Observation survey conducted at the very height of the blitz in November 1940, only 40 per cent of Londoners actually took shelter from the nightly bombing.

The majority of the population preferred to take their chances in their own beds, or under their own stairs! However, of those who took shelter, around four in every hundred went to the tube. With characteristic British stoicism, many of these 180,000 people queued during the day in order to ensure a place at night.

Although the blitz was nothing to sing about, it did generate at least one popular song. Composers Fred and Doris Fisher, perhaps because they were American and, consequently, far from the destruction and horror in London, produced the oddly titled song *Blitzkrieg Baby*. In its ambitious attempt at topicality through its references to '*blitzkrieg*', 'hand grenade', 'bombs', 'TNT', and sundry other paraphernalia of war, it was one of the less fortunate songs of the period. Its juxtaposition of sultry, love-song style

with the harsh reminders of war resulted in a curious paradox best appreciated by those who, like the composers, never experienced first-hand the horrors of war. The result was a rather nonsensical lyric that, nevertheless, was popular with many people when delivered by the velvet-voiced Una Mae Carlisle.

> *Blitzkrieg baby you can't bomb me,*
> *'Cause I'm pleading neutrality,*
> *Got my gun out, can't you see?*
> *Blitzkrieg baby you can't bomb me.*

It is surprising how quickly most people adapted to the blitz. By October 1940, barely a month after it had started, people were so blasé about the bombing that the newspapers reported that no one left the Wyndham Theatre when the sirens wailed. Indeed, in many theatres the bombing became almost part of the show, with the performers on stage inviting the audience to an informal singalong until the all-clear sounded. Many people emerged cheerfully from a night in the shelter to go to morning dances. A 23 November 1940 report in *Melody Maker* quoted the manager of the Plaza Ballroom, Derby, as saying that business had never been better than during the blitz and that he was actually turning away customers every Friday night! The manager went on to say: 'A few weeks ago I broke all records at a certain town in the Midlands, where 1,120 danced and really enjoyed themselves whilst bombs were dropping all around.' Happily, there

were relatively few dance-hall disasters. One of the worst occurred at London's Café de Paris, in Coventry Street, which killed thirty-four people, including band-leader Ken 'Snakehips' Johnson and members of his orchestra.

Despite such tragedies people continued to dance. They could not spend all their time sheltering from the blitz. Dancing was never more popular than during the war and many people literally danced through the blitz. Dance halls provided a temporary refuge from the bleak realities of war and rationing. They were places of innocent pleasure where, for a few hours at least, the anxieties and frustrations of the outside world could be replaced by the comfort of another's arms. While most women went to the dance halls for the simple enjoyment of dancing and comradeship, many lonely servicemen, often on only forty-eight-hour leave before returning to the front, had different ideas. Fast talking could be as important as fast footwork.

The dance halls attracted crowds that are almost unimaginable today. It was not uncommon for 10,000 customers a week to pack into a single dance hall. So popular was dancing that the bigger halls ran four separate sessions each day – a morning coffee dance, an afternoon tea dance, and two separate evening sessions. Uniformed members of the forces were usually admitted at half price – and were frequently provided with dancing shoes by dance-hall owners anxious to preserve

(LEFT): MEN (PARTICULARLY SOLDIERS ON LEAVE FROM THE FRONT) AND WOMEN BOTH SOUGHT ESCAPE FROM THE HARSH REALITIES OF WAR IN DANCE HALLS.

(BELOW): FROM OPERA TO JITTERBUG – EVEN THE COVENT GARDEN OPERA HOUSE SWUNG TO THE SOUNDS OF THE BIG BANDS.

their sprung floors from the heavy pounding of army boots! 'Forces-only' nights were also a frequent feature, to which female – but no male – civilians were admitted. Although the blitz temporarily closed many establishments, some, like the Hammersmith Palais in London, could echo the famous Windmill Theatre's boast that they never closed.

The jitterbug and jive, imported from the States, were the rage with energetic youngsters. Yet their frenetic activity was frequently disturbing to older dancers. The managers of many dance halls devised strategies to keep the jitter-buggers under control. One common device was to have a jitterbug competition – with attractive prizes – early in the evening. This not only kept the kids from running riot, but it so wore them out that the rest of the evening could be passed without interruption by the more sedate ballroom dancers doing their foxtrots, waltzes, quicksteps, tangos and other tra-ditional ballroom dances. Nevertheless, jitterbug was what the kids mostly came to do.

Community dances were also popular. High on the agenda of more tra-ditional exhibitionists was the Blackout Stroll. Other novelty dances included the Kangaroo Hop (in honour of our

Australian allies), the hokey-cokey, and Hands Knees Boomps-a-Daisy.

Latin dances – conga, rhumba – were very big during the war, stimulated, no doubt, by the fact that many of the imported wartime American musicals and comedies – to say nothing of the domestic theatrical revues – had Latin American locations – 'Saludos Amigos', 'The Mexican Spitfire', 'That Night in Rio' and 'Mexican Hayride'.

Even songs *about* dancing were popular. The engagingly entitled *Arthur Murray Taught Me Dancing in a Hurry* celebrated the master American dance teacher and the haste of his young pro-tégés to learn the latest dance steps before they were parted by the war. The even more imaginatively titled *Six Lessons from Madame La Zonga,* while putatively celebrating conga lessons, sometimes suffered from barrackroom ribaldry.

> *Her four latin daughters will help*
> *you to start,*
> *While finding the rhythm you might*
> *lose your heart…*
> *And…if Madame likes you,*
> *The lessons are free.*

Of course, not all dancing was done in dance halls. Dancing in the streets was not uncommon at this time. Not in celebration, but in defiance. Many were the photographs and newsreel pictures that showed Britons literally dancing on the rubble of their destroyed homes. In a show of scorn after that city was blitzed, the soldiers, sailors and civilians of Plymouth danced together on the Hoe while the docks still smouldered around them. In a famous headline, the *Daily Mirror* proclaimed 'Let the People Sing? You Can't Stop 'Em! over a photograph of Cockneys dancing and

THE RECORD-BREAKING FILM 'GONE WITH THE WIND' PLAYED FROM THE BLITZ RIGHT THROUGH TO D-DAY FOUR YEARS LATER.

singing in their devastated streets.

Cinemas adapted to the blitz by showing films at earlier times, and in the West End some people went straight from the shelters to queue for matinee tickets. The hottest ticket in town during the blitz was for 'Gone With the Wind', which resulted in the curious phenomenon of people emerging from the shelters to queue for tickets to see Atlanta burn. And although announcements were made or notices displayed on the screen whenever an air raid started, very few people left the cinema. Rhett and Scarlett's contribution to the raising of morale at this time cannot be overestimated. Scarlett's example of surviving the destruction of Tara and Atlanta gave heart to millions.

As the newsreels showed, the plucky Brits bore the blitz with their characteristic fortitude. No matter how many bombs the Germans rained down on them, they were seen grinning and bearing it; they smiled at the cameras and gave the Churchillian V-sign as they looked at the rubble that was once their homes. The now Queen Mother with her husband King George VI began what we now call 'walkabouts', meeting the people who had lost their houses, standing at the bomb-sites with them, chatting and consoling them, telling them that their main residence, Buckingham Palace, had not escaped the bombs; although it is hard to imagine how this would have eased the trauma of someone who had lost his or her entire home and most of his possessions. Nevertheless, during the war years these informal Royal conversations, which offered nothing more than sympathy and a kind word to victims of the blitz, made a significant mark on the collective psyche of the British public. It is no coincidence that the 'Queen Mum' is still regarded as the most popular of all the Royals. The deep and abiding affection that the public holds for her can be traced right back to how she mixed with the people in those dark days more than fifty years ago.

From the distance of so many years it is equally hard to understand the popularity of one of the great love songs written during the blitz. As is the case with *Blitzkrieg Baby*, there is a strange paradox in Bennie Benjemen and Eddie Durham's classic love song, *I Don't Want to Set the World on Fire*. It seems wholly inappropriate that this song, published in London at the height of the blitz, when the city was literally burning around them, could be successful. Yet it was.

> *I don't want to set the world on fire,*
> *I just want to start a flame in your heart.*
> *In my heart I have but one desire,*
> *And that one is you, no other will do.*

Melody Maker, the leading magazine for popular music, reported that throughout the war years dance-band music was booming. This was not just in London, where resident hotel and nightclub bands were consistently playing to packed

GLENN MILLER, PLAYING TROMBONE, FRONTING HIS CIVILIAN BAND BEFORE CREATING HIS LEGENDARY AEF (AMERICAN EXPEDITIONARY FORCES) ORCHESTRA.

audiences, but in other towns and cities throughout Britain as well. For example, Joe Loss and His Orchestra attracted more than 10,000 paying customers during a week's engagement at Glasgow's Playhouse Ballroom, and other bandleaders and musicians reported similar record-breaking attendances everywhere.

At the same time, some bandleaders were being regarded as heroes. Not only Major Glenn Miller, of course, but also Geraldo – real name Gerald Bright – who was appointed Supervisor of the ENSA Band Division, and who took most of the members of the highly popular Savoy Hotel Orchestra on a tour of the Middle East. And indeed, the dance-band profession did suffer its casualties, both from active service on the front line and from bombing raids at home. Crooner Al Bowlly, 'the British Bing Crosby', was killed on 17 April 1941 when a land mine fell outside the block of flats in which he lived; whilst just a few weeks earlier bandleader, Ken 'Snakehips'

Johnson and his tenor saxman, Dave Williams, were blown to bits by a direct hit on London's number-one 'nite spot' the Café de Paris. The irony of this tragedy was that right at the time the bomb fell, the band were playing the Hugh Charles and Louis Elton hit, *When They Sound the Last All-Clear.*

> *When they sound the last All-Clear,*
> *How happy, my darling, we'll be...*
> *And the whole world will sing,*
> *When they sound the last All-Clear.*

CHAPTER SIX

The Turning Tide: North Africa, Stalingrad and D-Day

Lili Marlene

THE DARK DAYS of the Battle of Britain and the blitz were not without their brighter moments. One shaft of light in the otherwise unremitting gloom came in December 1940, when the Greeks unexpectedly turned back the invading Italian armies. Not only did Mussolini's Fascists get their noses bloodied, but the Duce himself became the butt of a rollicking song. To commemorate the surprise Greek victory Phil Park penned new lyrics to Nino Casiroli's song *Evviva la Torre di Pisa*. The resulting song, *Oh! What a Surprise for the Duce*, quickly became the backbone of many a singalong.

> *Poor Mussolini*
> *Has got just a teeny bit*
> *Suspicious he's made a mistake.*
> *Saying the Mediterranean*
> *Was an Italian lake.*

GENERAL MONTGOMERY AT EL ALAMEIN, NOVEMBER 1942: THE FIRST ALLIED LAND VICTORY.

*O-h! What a
surprise for the
Du-ce, the Du-ce,
He can't put it over
the Greeks.
O-h! What a surprise for the Du-ce,
they say
He's had no spaghetti for weeks.*

THE 'DESERT FOX' – FIELD MARSHAL ROMMEL, COMMANDER OF THE DEFEATED GERMAN AFRIKA CORPS IN 1942.

Unfortunately, the plucky Greek resistance was soon overwhelmed when the Germans went to the aid of their Italian allies. For the Western Allies it would be almost another two years before they had something to cheer about. It would take the defeat of the Desert Fox by the Desert Rats to raise British spirits.

It was only after the Allied victories in North Africa in November 1942 and at Stalingrad a month later that the myth of Nazi invincibility began to crumble. People at last began to see light at the end of the tunnel and started to think – and sing – of future victory. Hubert Gregg's *I'm Gonna Get Lit-Up* was written for George Black's musical 'Strike a New Note' and introduced to the nation by the bubbly Zoë Gail in 1943. Anticipating future celebration, the song begins with the words:

*When somebody shouts 'The fight's up!'
And 'It's time to put the lights up!'
Then the first thing to be lit-up will be me.*

By the end of the war *I'm Gonna Get Lit Up* was one of the most popular victory songs.

There was really something to sing about when the British 8th Army, led by General Montgomery, soundly beat the crack Afrika Korps of Field Marshal Rommel at El Alamein in November 1942. It was the Allies' first major land victory over the German army and people everywhere celebrated the defeat of the Desert Fox (as Rommel was called) by Monty's stalwart Desert Rats. Churchill, in celebrating the victory, set British hearts soaring with those wonderfully ambiguous words: 'This is not the end; it is not even the beginning of the end, but it is, perhaps, the end of the beginning...' For the first time since the disaster in France and Dunkirk, there was now a real conviction that the Allies not only could, but would, win the war.

Oddly enough, the song most closely associated with this period, was a German one. It was called *Lili Marlene*. The song was first recorded in a German studio by singer Lale Anderson. Its original title hardly set the pulses of red-blooded males racing – it was called *Song of a*

'We Are Not Interested in the Possibilities of Defeat...' *

AUXILIARY FIRE SERVICE

AFS
LONDON NEEDS AUXILIARY FIREMEN **NOW**

FRANK NEWBOULD

ENROL AT ANY FIRE STATION
CIVIL DEFENCE

* – Queen Victoria in December 1899, during the Boer War. This quotation was framed by Winston Churchill and placed on his desk in the War Cabinet Rooms for the duration of the Second World War, where it can still be seen today.

(LEFT): IN SPITE OF ALL THE OBSTACLES IMPOSED BY THE BLACKOUT, THE TRAINS, FOR THE MOST PART, DID RUN ON TIME.

(BELOW): THE PROPAGANDA CARTOON CHARACTER THE 'SQUANDER BUG' WAS CREATED TO MAKE HOUSEWIVES, ESPECIALLY, FEEL GUILTY IF THEY PURCHASED ANYTHING BUT ESSENTIAL GOODS.

(PREVIOUS PAGE): OF ALL THE ESSENTIAL WAR WORK CARRIED OUT ON THE HOME FRONT, THE FIRE-FIGHTING SERVICE WAS UNDOUBTEDLY TOP OF THE LIST. RECRUITING FOR VOLUNTEERS CONTINUED FOR THE DURATION.

"My girl's a WOW"

WOMAN ORDNANCE WORKER

CIVIL DEFENCE
WOMEN WANTED FOR
EVACUATION SERVICE

OFFER YOUR SERVICES
TO YOUR LOCAL COUNCIL
OR ANY BRANCH OF WOMEN'S VOLUNTARY SERVICES

NATIONAL

Keep mum she's not so dumb!

(ABOVE): THIS POSTER,
AIMED AT YOUNG
WOMEN IN PARTICULAR,
WAS A POTENT IMAGE
THAT HELPED TO
RECRUIT THOUSANDS
INTO WAR WORK.

(ABOVE):
SURROGATE
MOTHERING
WAS GREATLY
ENCOURAGED
BY THE GOVERN-
MENT TO EASE
THE PAIN AND
BEWILDERMENT OF
CHILDREN SENT TO
NEW HOMES AND
FAMILIES.

(LEFT): THROUGHOUT
THE WAR, POSTERS OF
THE 'CARELESS TALK
COSTS LIVES' VARIETY
CONSTANTLY WARNED OF
THE ENEMY WITHIN.

'Play it Again Sam...'

It's A Lovely Day Tomorrow
WORDS & MUSIC BY IRVING BERLIN

(RIGHT): ONE OF THE SONGS OF OPTIMISM THAT LOOKED FORWARD TO A BRIGHTER TOMORROW WHEN THE DEVASTATION OF WAR WOULD FINALLY END.

(BELOW): FRANK (THE VOICE) SINATRA WITH A SONG THAT CREATED THE VERY FIRST BOBBYSOXERS ON BOTH SIDES OF THE ATLANTIC.

I COULDN'T SLEEP A WINK LAST NIGHT
Words by HAROLD ADAMSON Music by JIMMY McHUGH
RECORDED BY FRANK SINATRA
CHAPPELL & CO., LTD.
59, NEW BOND STREET, LONDON, W.1.

LONDON I CANNOT LEAVE YOU
WORDS BY KIERAN TUNNEY
MUSIC BY LORD FOLEY

(ABOVE): NOT THE ANTHEM OF TENS OF THOUSANDS OF LONDON'S EVACUEES — ALTHOUGH IT EXPRESSED THE SADNESS OF MANY OF ITS INHABITANTS WHO WERE FORCED TO LEAVE THE CITY.

(RIGHT): THE GLENN MILLER INSTRUMENTAL THAT HE DEDICATED TO HIS WIFE, HELEN, FEATURED IN THE POST-WAR FILM 'THE GLENN MILLER STORY', STARRING JAMES STEWART AND JUNE ALLYSON.

(ABOVE): THERE WERE NOT TOO MANY PET RABBITS RUNNING AROUND DURING THE WAR — THE SHORTAGE OF MEAT SAW TO THAT.

(RIGHT): AN IMMENSELY POPULAR SONG, BOTH IN THE USA AND IN BRITAIN, TO WHICH EVERY SERVICEMAN COULD RELATE. IT WAS FEATURED IN THE 1943 FILM 'SOMETHING TO SHOUT ABOUT', STARRING DON AMECHE AND JANET BLAIR.

'If I Had a Talking Picture of You...'

(ABOVE): AFTER A STRING OF EALING COMEDY HITS, ALEC GUINNESS MADE HIS MARK AS AN INTERNATIONAL STAR IN THIS EPIC FILM DIRECTED BY DAVID LEAN IN 1957. THE STORY WAS BASED ON A TRUE WARTIME EXPERIENCE.

(RIGHT): IN THIS 1942 FILM, GREER GARSON WAS MRS MINIVER TO MILLIONS OF WARTIME MOVIE-GOERS. SHE EPITOMISED BRITISH MIDDLE-CLASS STOICISM IN THE FACE OF ADVERSITY, AND WALTER PIDGEON WAS EVERY WOMAN'S DREAM OF A LOVING, SUPPORTIVE HUSBAND.

(BELOW): WILL HAY (STARRING HERE IN 'THE GOOSE STEPS OUT', IN 1942) WAS REGARDED BY THE MOST DISCERNING BRITISH CINEMA–GOERS AS THEIR FINEST CELLULOID COMEDIAN.

(RIGHT): 'LADY HAMILTON', MADE IN 1941, WAS SAID TO BE WINSTON CHURCHILL'S FAVOURITE FILM – NOT LEAST, PERHAPS, BECAUSE HE CONTRIBUTED TO PARTS OF THE SCRIPT.

(BELOW): THE 1939 FILM THAT WILL BE FOREVER ASSOCIATED WITH JUDY GARLAND AND THE MAGIC SHE CREATED AS DOROTHY, THE LITTLE GIRL FROM KANSAS.

(NEXT PAGE): 'CASABLANCA' HAS A PERMANENT PLACE IN EVERY FILM BUFF'S TOP TEN OF ALL–TIME GREAT MOVIES.

THE ORIGINAL LAMP-LIGHT GIRL, LALE ANDERSON, SINGING HER HIT *LILLI MARLENE*.

Young Sentry. As a consequence, it sold just over 600 copies, and seemed doomed for the shellac scrapyard, where the remaining unsold discs might have been reconstituted into other nationally required products. But then, in 1941, Germany invaded Yugoslavia and the powerful Belgrade radio transmitter became just another outlet for Dr Goebbels' Propaganda Ministry. As the Belgrade transmitter was the closest to the German armies in North Africa, it became the main source of radio signals for Rommel's Afrika Korps. However, it was still staffed by Yugoslavians who were carefully vetted to ensure that they were loyal to the Third Reich. The question was, what were they to play? The radio producers searched their sound archives in an effort to find suitable German popular music, but all they could come up with was some very old Serbo-Croat songs, so they made an urgent request to Radio Vienna to send them some of the very latest German records. The plea was duly acknowledged, and an assorted bunch of discs was sent to Radio Belgrade, including the 'smash flop' *Song of a Young Sentry*. Then fate intervened again as one of the station's presenters referred to the song as *Lili Marlene* (or, more properly, *Lili Marleen*, as it is spelt in

German). This time it took off, particularly at first with Rommel's men, who were within range of the powerful Belgrade transmitter.

Monty's men of the 8th Army also liked the tune and began to sing the song, giving it the perhaps unique distinction of being a song that was sung with equal gusto by members of opposing armies. The British government was, however, concerned about its squaddies singing a German song and commissioned Tin Pan Alley songwriter Tommy Connor (who had had previous successes with *The Biggest Aspidistra in the World* and *Chestnut Tree*) to rewrite the lyrics. It is Connor's version that has come down to us in the recordings from the war.

You Must Remember This...

*Underneath the lantern by the barrack
gate,
Darling, I remember the way you used to
wait.
It was there that you whispered tenderly,
That you loved me.
You'll always be,
My own Lili Marlene.*

Connor's version was first recorded in English by an ex-Ambrose singer, seventeen-year-old Anne Shelton, and became a huge British hit. Later, Marlene Dietrich made a recording in the USA and it became a permanent part of her highly acclaimed cabaret act. Nor did its recording history end there: in Italy it was belted out by operatic tenors to Mussolini's reluctant soldiers. 'Lili' the lamplight girl is now immortalised in the popular music 'hall of fame' andthe origi-

nal writers, Hans Leip and Norbert Schultz, due to Englishman Tommy Connor, saw their disc disaster turn into a top-ten triumph. It was, without doubt, the song most redolent of the war.

There were, however, versions of *Lili Marlene* other than Tommy Connor's. Even before Connor had rewritten the lyric, the Tommies of Monty's Desert Rats had produced lyrics of their own for this real song of the desert – some bawdy and some respectable. One British 8th Army version began:

*There was a song that the Eighth Army
used to hear,
In the lonely desert, lovely, sweet and clear.
Over the ether came the strain, the soft
refrain each night again,
With you, Lili Marlene – with you, Lili
Marlene.*

After the defeat of the Afrika Korps a more rowdy version became popular in pubs and barrackrooms:

*Afrika Korps has vanished from the earth,
Smashed soon the swine that gave it birth,
No more we'll hear that lilting strain, that
soft refrain, each night again,
With you, Lili Marlene – with you,
Lily Marlene.*

Monty's great British desert campaign,

The Turning Tide

coupled with the almost simultaneous counteroffensive by the Russian army on the German Panzer divisions at Stalingrad, has been acknowledged by most historians as the real turning point of the Second World War. Until Operation Barbarossa, the German surprise attack on the Soviet Union in June 1941, the Germans and Russians had maintained an uneasy accommodation with each other. This was shattered when the Germans attacked. The Russians suffered appalling losses as they fell back to defensive positions around Stalingrad and Moscow. By December the tide had turned and Russian might (aided by the Russian winter) had dealt the Germans their second land defeat. Suddenly the Russians, whom Churchill secretly regarded with almost as much mistrust and apprehension as the Germans, had fought and won an heroic battle. So whatever Churchill felt about Joseph Stalin, he certainly kept quiet about it at this time, and encouraged the mood of victory in Britain which was reflected by pictures of smiling Russian soldiers waving their rifles triumphantly in the newspapers, whilst newsreel commentators referred to the victorious soldiers rounding up the despondent blizzard-bitten German remnants of an army as 'Ivan'. This term of affection was used in much the same way as the collective word 'Tommy' was for all British soldiers in the ranks or 'Joe' for GIs.

At this time there was a flurry of popular songs to honour the success of the Russian allies. *My Katrina, Mission to Moscow, The Red Cavalry March* and *Russian Rose* were just some of those with Russian themes to hit the airwaves at this time. *Ya Vass Loublyu (Means I Love You)* commemorated, perhaps a touch over-intimately, the new state of relations between the Allied forces. Glenn Miller played his own tribute to the Russians with a swing version of the traditional *Volga Boatman's Song*, and other big bands on both sides of the Atlantic brought out new arrangements of the Russian love song *Hortche Chornya (Dark Eyes)*, that of Harry Roy and His Band being perhaps the most exuberant of the British versions.

> Little Russian maid,
> Do not be afraid,
> For tomorrow may bring back yesterday...
> You are haunting me, dear Dark Eyes.

After the turning-of-the-tide period in Russia and Egypt, the phrase 'the Second Front is coming soon' was in regular parlance among servicemen in the war zones and civilians back home. Everyone knew that the invasion of Europe had to come. The question on everyone's lips was: when? In the event it was almost another eighteen months before D-Day actually occurred. So there was much preparation and planning ahead and a massive build-up of men and materials. Many of the victorious 8th Army men who had been joined by the less experienced 1st Army were sent back to England for the begin-

You Must Remember This...

(Left): An ENSA mobile cinema unit prepares for a packed house of servicemen 'somewhere in France'.

(Below): Sgt Marius Goring (in polka dots), later to become a leading cinema actor, showed an emerging talent as part of 'The Saucy Queens' concert party of the 14th Queen's Royal Regiment.

ning of manoeuvres for Operation Overlord, whilst the Americans, whose numbers were increasing all the time in Britain, were gearing up for the big battle.

The concentration of troops in Britain as they prepared for D -Day caused enormous problems. Troop morale and discipline were of constant concern and one way to keep the soldiers happy was to provide them with plenty of entertainments. In many ways this was the golden age of ENSA as its shows, and the mobile cinemas it ran for the troops, were in constant demand. Yet because of the

huge strain put on ENSA personnel and resources at this time a new form of entertaining the troops at home and abroad emerged. The government decided that a fund would be made available to unit commanders for the servicemen and women to put on their own shows. It was probably from this time onwards that Britain first developed the unique admiration for amateur performers which persists to this day. The efforts of these makeshift concert-party groups were much appreciated by service audiences and indeed some did produce stars of the future who, until they found themselves almost reluctantly thrust into these theatrical activities, had no idea that they had any special talents. Among these amateur entertainers were the founding members of the Goons: Leading Aircraftsman Peter Sellers, Lance Bombardier Harry Secombe and Gunner Terence Alan Milligan, later nicknamed 'Spike' after his musician idol, Spike Hughes. Their innovative radio comedy programme, 'The Goon Show', captivated the nation during the 1950s with its unique style of surrealistic humour. Widely considered by modern comedy performers and the public alike as a watershed in British comedy, the Goons went on to become British legends, influencing generations of performers for decades afterwards.

The build-up of troops and equipment preparatory to the reconquest of Europe continued throughout the winter of 1943 and the spring of 1944. On 6 June 1944, the time had come at last. It was D-Day and the long-awaited invasion of Europe by an enormous Allied fighting force was underway: the American 1st Army and the British 2nd Army reached the beaches of Normandy and slowly gained ground between Le Havre and Cherbourg. The song that typified that 'calm before the storm' period, *Cleanin' My Rifle and Dreaming of You,* written by Allie Wrubel, now seemed a bit redundant, with all weaponry blazing constantly as the Allied forces were eventually able to spread out across France and push the Germans back to the Rhine. In the process, and as a token gesture, a platoon of British soldiers did actually wash some underwear and hang it out on the Siegfried Line. But, strangely, the songs that emanated from the radio now were not, as might have been expected, of the 'we've-got-the- Hun-on-the-run' variety. Instead, it was the nonsensical songs that became huge hits – perhaps as a reaction to the horrors and stresses of war. Whatever the reason, the songwriters kept churning them out. The most successful of this batch was the infectious *Maizy Doats and Dozy Doats* with words and music by Milton Drake, Al Hoffman and Jerry Livingston.

> *Maizy doats and dozy doats*
> *And liddle lambzy divey.*
> *A kiddle-y divey too,*
> *Wouldn't you?*

CHAPTER SEVEN

The Home Front

If I Had Lots of Coupons

ECAUSE BRITAIN came within six weeks of running out of food during the First World War, preparations for rationing were well in hand even before the first shot was fired in the Second. The Ministry of Food – which employed 50,000 civil servants – organized rationing (and the huge bureaucracy of ration books, identity cards, and all the other paraphernalia it took to run it).

Rationing was introduced gradually. Only days into the war, on 22 September 1939, the first item to be rationed was petrol. Private motorists were rationed according to need, with those requiring

the most petrol being limited to just 10 gallons of 'pool' petrol *per month*. (Those with a lesser call on the nation's supplies received a monthly ration of just 4 gallons.) However, even with such a miserly allocation it was not possible to conserve fuel supplies, so on 1 July 1942 motoring for pleasure was abolished altogether. After that date only essential users, such as

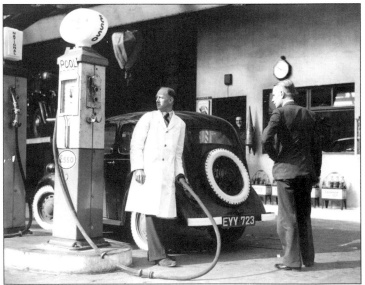

IT MAY HAVE BEEN 1/6D PER GALLON BUT VERY FEW PEOPLE WERE LEGALLY ENTITLED TO BUY PETROL.

Rations

Sept '39	Petrol	
Jan '40	Bacon, ham & butter	4 oz per week
	Sugar	12 oz per week
March '40	Meat	1/10d (9pence) per adult/week
July '40	Tea, margarine and cooking fats	2 oz per week
March '41	Jam, mince, syrup, marmalade, honey	4 oz per week
June '41	Cheese, clothes	
Sept '42	Ice-cream	Prohibited for the duration (except on American bases)

IT WAS STILL SMILES AS BRITAIN TIGHTENED ITS BELT AND RATION BOOKS WERE DISTRIBUTED ACROSS THE LAND.

doctors, received a small allowance.

Some items – fish, vegetables, sausages – were never rationed (although shortages meant that huge queues developed whenever it was rumoured that a fresh supply had come in).

One consequence of shortages was that the Ministry of Food introduced new foods and fish not previously eaten by most people. Spam and snook, for example, graced the nation's tables for the first time during the war and the Ministry went to great lengths to popularize them. Newsreel 'Food Facts' in the cinema and the BBC Radio wartime cooking programme 'The Kitchen Front' encouraged people to experiment with

ELSIE AND DORIS WATERS (BETTER KNOWN
TO THEIR MILLIONS OF BBC LISTENERS AS
'GERT' AND 'DAISY') GIVE A
DEMONSTRATION OF WARTIME COOKERY.

the new foods, as well as providing new recipes for old ones. Lord Woolton, the Minister of Food, proved almost as popular as the cartoon character Potato Pete in driving home the need for rationing. As the war progressed, more cartoon characters – Clara Carrot, Doctor Carrot – were introduced to help reinforce the need (and means) for good nutrition. Together with Lord Woolton, they helped make the situation palatable.

The Ministry of Food found new and wholesome – but not necessarily appetizing – things to do with available food resources (primarily potatoes, carrots, beets, and turnips). Lord Woolton himself was immortalized when his name was given to a pie that consisted entirely of vegetables (potatoes, turnips, carrots) and oats in a pastry crust. The humble carrot became the mainstay of many a diet and there were recipes for carrot marmalade, carrot pie, carrot flan and carrot cake. The revelation that RAF

MICKEY MOUSE PRESENTS THE
NEW DISNEY CARTOON
CREATION, CLARA CARROT, TO
BRITAIN'S MINISTER OF FOOD,
LORD WOOLTON.

pilots, the glamour boys of the services, ate carrots to improve their night vision was not entirely unconnected with the Ministry's drive to make vegetables more attractive to schoolchildren. That adults might also conclude that improved night vision was useful in blackout conditions was, of course, coincidental. There were also information campaigns to encourage people to eat potato skins and bread crusts as it was drummed into them time and again that 'food is a munition of war'.

The necessity of a system of rationing to ensure the equal distribution of foodstuffs was widely accepted, but was, nevertheless, a sore trial for many people. In order to alleviate the more draconian aspects of rationing, 'points rationing' was introduced in December 1941. In this system each adult was allocated sixteen points (later twenty) each month to 'spend' on foods of their choice.

Difficulties with transport and supplies meant that even foods that were not rationed were often in short supply. Fish, for example, rarely made it to the Midlands, and fresh eggs were 'allocated' rather than actually rationed. However, the shortage of hens (many of which found their way into the cooking pot because of the strict rations on meat) meant that only expectant mothers, infants and invalids had an adequate supply of eggs. The war placed a huge burden on the British economy. As part of the Lend-Lease programme (which enabled Britain to buy foodstuffs from America on credit), the USA began, in 1942, to supply powdered eggs to supplement the British diet, but like those other imported foods from America, spam and powdered milk, they were not received with relish.

EVERYBODY NEEDS GOOD NEIGHBOURS. TO HELP DURING A FUEL SHORTAGE, BAKER MR PRICE COOKS DINNERS FOR HOUSEWIVES AND DISTRIBUTES THEM OVER THE GARDEN WALL.

Introduced to near universal derision, they were, nevertheless, an essential addition at a time when the ration of fresh milk was just two and a half pints each week – and each adult averaged but a single egg each fortnight! Yet the failure of powdered egg and powdered milk to make a satisfactory Yorkshire pudding forever poisoned these products in many cooks' eyes.

A number of gently ironic songs that marked the adversity of rationing were produced at this time. By the time Ralph Butler and Noel Gay's *Hey! Little Hen!* was published in 1941, eggs had already become an increasingly rare luxury. As a result, many people resorted to keeping chickens in the back garden in order to supplement both their meat ration and their egg allocation. Yet all too often the hens failed to deliver. So the smiles the song produced were tempered with a sympathetic understanding of the singer's plea that the one surviving chicken should lay an egg for tea.

> *I had a lot of chickens,*
> *A large chicken run,*
> *But owing to conditions,*
> *I'm now down to one.*

> *Hey, little hen, when, when, when*
> *Will you lay me an egg for my tea?*
> *Hey, little hen, when, when, when,*
> *Will you try to supply one for me?*

Another popular song relating to food rationing was similarly lighthearted. In the near meatlessness of rationing, rabbit – which was not rationed – assumed a new prominence. Many people raised rabbits in garden hutches, and rabbit hunting (and poaching) provided significant supplements to many people's diets. An earlier effort about rabbits by songwriter Noel Gay – who came close to being in the George Formby bracket as a morale-booster, having composed a seemingly endless supply of inventive and romantic songs throughout the Second World War – went through several incarnations during the course of the war.

Noel Gay's *Run, Rabbit, Run!* (originally written for the show 'The Little Dog Laughed', which opened in October 1939, before food rationing was introduced) owed its original success not to the send-up of rationing, but rather to the parody lyrics popularized by the show's stars, Flanagan and Allen. In place of the lyric exhorting a rabbit to fleet-footedly flee the farmer's gun,

> *Run, rabbit, run, rabbit,*
> *Run, run, run.*
> *Run, rabbit, run, rabbit,*
> *Run, run, run.*
> *Bang, bang, bang, bang,*
> *Goes the farmer's gun.*
> *Run, rabbit, run, rabbit,*
> *Run, run, run.*

Flanagan and Allen substituted some highly topical references which captured the mood of the nation during the Phoney War period.

Run, Adolf, run, Adolf, run, run, run,
Look what you've been gone and done,
    done, done.
We will knock the stuffing out of you,
Field Marshal Goering and Goebbels too.
You'll lose your place in the sun, sun, sun.
Soon, you poor dog, you'll get none,
    none, none.
You will flop with Herr von Ribbentrop,
So, run, Adolf, run, Adolf, run, run, run.

Another early parody verse went:

Run, Adolf, run, Adolf, run, run, run,
Now that the fun has begun, 'gun, 'gun.
P'raps you'll just allow us to explain,
What we did once we can do again.
We're making shells by the ton, ton, ton,
We've got the hun on the run, run, run.
Poor old soul, you'll need a rabbit hole,
So run, Adolf, run, Adolf, run, run, run.

The song's original lyric got a second life when a news item highlighted a story about how a marauding Luftwaffe plane had killed some rabbits in the Shetlands. Then, still later in the war, as rationing began to pinch, the original lyric took on a new level of poignancy. Finally, showing the versatility of the song, the parody lyrics were yet again sung with renewed glee after the Allied victories in North Africa and Stalingrad in the winter of 1942–43.

Regardless of which version of *Run, Rabbit, Run!* was current, the sad fact remained that on the Home Front the shortages, of food in particular, were

hitting hard. It was not only meat that was in short supply. German and Japanese submarine warfare severely affected the shipping of food supplies from overseas. Tropical fruits – oranges and bananas – were particularly scarce as a result. While the Americans made up some of the deficit by shipping over huge quantities of orange juice, large queues continued to form whenever oranges appeared. And so rare were bananas that a whole generation of children were growing up having never seen, let alone eaten, one.

Many are the stories, not all apocryphal, of children who tried to eat the skin when bananas reappeared in 1946. There are stories, too, of various pranks revolving around the reappearance of the banana. At one boarding school, for example, the older students told the younger ones, who had never seen a banana, to save the skins so that they could be refilled. At the end of the meal the young schoolboys solemnly handed in the skins to their bemused schoolmaster. As the band leader Harry Roy plaintively sang:

The one thing I always crave,
And that's why you hear me sing,
Oh, when can I have a banana again?

Nor was it only children who had to do without. Although not rationed, cigarettes were scarce. The high cost and irregularity of supplies meant that many people bought cigarettes two or three at a time. This shortage was observed in a

parody song that lists favourite brands, sung to the tune of *You are My Sunshine*.

> *You are my sunshine,*
> *My Double Woodbine,*
> *My box of matches,*
> *My Craven A.*

In the face of food shortages many people began, quite literally, to grow their own. People turned to their 'victory gardens' and allotments with vigour. Numerous songs encouraged self-sufficiency and their titles – *Go to it!*, *Dig, Dig, Dig for Victory* and even *Up Housewives and at 'Em* – give a clear indication of their intent.

Such exhortations evidently did the job as home-grown produce helped fill an important gap. Without any doubt this must have helped to improve the health of the nation – but there were still luxuries that were hankered after. Sweets and chocolates, of course, but there were also other items never previously regarded as luxuries that were now in desperately short supply. Chief among these were clothes.

The rationing of clothes began in June 1941. Under the points system for clothing each adult initially received sixty-six coupons (later cut to forty-eight and then to just forty coupons per year). A woollen dress 'cost' eleven points and an overcoat eighteen. As a result, many strategies were devised to make the ration last. People 'bought big' and 'turned down' in order to meet the requirements of growing children – far preferable to hand-me-downs.

With a mere handkerchief costing

AS MR MIDDLETON, THE BBC'S WARTIME GARDENING EXPERT, WOULD SAY: 'THE ANSWER'S IN THE SOIL.'

The Home Front

three coupons, the pressure to conserve cloth was enormous. Unnecessary frills such as cuffs, flaps on pockets and trouser turn-ups disappeared and hemlines rose to just below the knee as clothing became more plain and practical. January 1942 saw the first examples of wartime Utility Clothing appear in the shops. These were cheap and simple, but well-made and durable, clothes. The standard outfit for women, a two-piece suit in hard-wearing tweed, became so popular that it was, according to *Vogue,* 'almost a civilian uniform'. These suits were given a new look each day through the judicious alternation of different blouses and accessories.

As with 'The Kitchen Front', the government had its own character, 'Mrs Sew and Sew', to provide helpful hints on how to stretch clothing allowances.

Women's magazines also ran columns which showed ways to turn even the most unpromising materials into useful clothing. In order to conserve cloth further, the government mounted advertising campaigns that encouraged people to 'make do and mend'. Cloth was recycled: worn-out parachute silk, for example, made excellent underwear. It became patriotic to have patches and, following the example of the frequently boiler-suited Mr Churchill, dress standards were relaxed. Because leather was scarce, wooden-soled shoes and even clogs came back into fashion. And because stockings were increasingly unavailable, many women went without.

Silk stockings had disappeared by

You Must Remember This…

early 1941. Submarine warfare had disrupted the supply of silk from the East, while the requirements of map and parachute makers took precedence over those of the fashion industry. Artificial silk stockings appeared about this time, but nylons proved almost as impossible to find – except in the American bases' post stores. An alternative was found in various forms of leg make-up and other forms of body paints that were designed specifically for the purpose. When applied, these gave the appearance of stockings – with a seam pencilled in with an eyebrow pencil. Many of those who could not afford leg make-up used cold coffee – which was not rationed. Leg coverings of another sort also became popular during the war years as the wearing of trousers by women became widely acceptable.

Cosmetics were also increasingly hard to find. Soap went on the ration in February 1942, and the amount of cosmetics available in the shops was only a quarter of the prewar level. Women's magazines again stepped into the breach with helpful tips about how to make one's own cosmetics: beetroot preparations were suggested as substitutes for lipstick while concoctions of powdered iris root were said to be useful as a dry shampoo.

The rationing of clothes generated its own wry songs. As always, the songwriters captured the moment with a string of lyrics that summed up a particular aspect of wartime experience. One of the lesser known songs was Alf Ritter's *If I Had Lots of Coupons (I'd Be a Millionaire)*. Sung by comedian Max Miller, it bemoaned the fact that no matter how much money one had, without coupons one couldn't buy clothes.

> *Now I've got lots of money,*
> *But that doesn't mean a thing…*
> *…But if I had lots of coupons,*
> *Then I'd be a millionaire!*

Coupons and ration books helped ensure that the burden of rationing was shared out equally while comic songs such as these helped lightened the load.

CHAPTER EIGHT

The Women's War

Rosie the Riveter

ALTHOUGH THE BURDEN of rationing fell hardest on women, this is not to imply that women spent the war concerned solely with cooking, sewing and making ersatz cosmetics. Most were not so lucky. Because millions of men had left their jobs to join the armed forces, there was a critical shortage of labour in the nation's factories. In an effort to plug this gap, the Minister of Labour, Ernest Bevin, said in March 1941: 'Transfer of women from their home is one of the biggest industrial problems of the war.' One consequence of this was that a huge campaign to encourage women to take up war work voluntarily was launched.

The initial take-up to

WOMEN FACTORY WORKERS THREW FASHION TO THE WINDS, DONNING BOILER SUITS AND SMILES ON THEIR WAY TO WAR WORK.

Bevin's call was slow, not least because of the radical solution it proposed. Prior to the war, it was unusual for women to work outside the home. Even female secretaries and shop assistants were comparatively rare on the eve of the war. But because the wartime labour situation was so acute measures more radical even than Bevin's call for volunteers were required. Thus, by the end of the year, conscription was introduced for single women and childless widows between the ages of twenty and thirty. (Later it was extended to women between eighteen and fifty-one years of age.)

Most women were not conscripted into the women's services (which usually had enough volunteers) but into essential war work – mostly armaments and munitions factories, but also shipyards and aircraft factories. So successful was the call that by April 1943 90 per cent of all single women between the ages of eighteen and forty were either in uniform or in industry. Even Princess Elizabeth joined the ATS (Auxiliary Territorial Service) to do her part.

> *She's part of the assembly line.*
> *She's making history,*
> *Working for Victory,*
> *Rosie – brrrrrrrrrrrr – the riveter.*

It was not only single women who answered the call. Although married women were not required to work outside the home, many chose to do so –

either out of patriotism or simply for the extra wages to help make ends meet. This was in direct contrast to Nazi Germany, where women were never fully mobilized. For this reason, it would not be too great an overstatement to say that it was women who won the war. Only when one remembers that on top of their war work most women still had to feed and clothe their families in the face of severe shortages, and cope with the strains and problems of losing their men to the forces, their children to evacuation, and their homes to the blitz, that the true debt owed to Britain's women can be recognized.

The importance of those working

Women

IT WAS SAID THAT THERE WAS MORE SCARCE FRUIT ON CARMEN MIRANDA'S TURBAN THAN IN ALL THE GREENGROCERS IN LONDON DURING THE WAR.

Women served in every branch of the armed forces. The ATS, WAAF (Women's Auxiliary Air Force), WRNS (Women's Royal Naval Service, more commonly known as Wrens), and WVS (Women's Voluntary Services for Civil Defence) played a vital role in the national war effort. In some cases women filled 'traditional' roles (i.e. making and distributing blankets, clothes and bandages for refugees and hospitals); but in many others they undertook roles not formerly associated with women (e.g. driving vehicles and crewing harbour launches, operating searchlights and aiming – but not firing – anti-aircraft guns). Women worked as radio operators and despatch riders. Some, like Amy Johnson, Britain's multi-record-breaking female pilot, even flew planes from the factories to the air bases. Women proved themselves adaptable for any kind of work, and in many cases were better than the men they replaced. Women workers excelled at jobs that involved

LAND GIRLS RELAXING AFTER A HARD DAY IN THE FIELDS.

concentration or precision. Many of these jobs were dangerous, but women were still kept from an active role in the fighting. Only members of the Women's Home Defence Corps were trained to shoot.

Women also filled the more traditional role of nurse. Their ministrations were greatly appreciated by the wounded, who, if the lyric of Art Noel and Don Pelosi's song *Nursie! Nursie!* is to be believed, were still well enough to exert a little emotional blackmail:

> *Nursie, come over here and hold*
> *my hand,*
> *Nursie, there's something I can't*
> *understand,*
> *Round my heart I've got a funny pain.*
> *Oh! Oh! Oh! Oh! it's coming on again.*
> *Nursie, come over and hold my hand,*
> *I feel awful shy.*

THERE WAS NO SHORTAGE OF WOMEN VOLUNTEERS TO THE FORCES.

> *Nursie, when I look at you,*
> *My heart goes goo-goo-goo.*
> *Nursie, nursie, I'm getting worsie*
> *What-cha gonna do?*

Although the war years were a time of liberation for many women, the new freedoms generated new problems as well as new responsibilities. With greater freedom as well as independent incomes, many women escaped from the traditional confines of the home. The phenomenon of 'shelter girls' and other liberating behaviour resulted in some degree of backlash. This can be seen most vividly in one of the government's information campaigns in which a Mata Hari-like figure graced a poster that warned: 'Keep Mum, She's Not So Dumb'.

In posters like this and the many others produced at the time, women were portrayed as the weakest link in the war effort. But such a portrayal was both unfair and inaccurate – prompted more, perhaps, by an unconscious fear of women's increasing liberation than of the realities of war.

CHAPTER NINE

Workers' Playtime

Let the People Sing

THE CALL TO ARMS mobilized the nation. By the end of 1942, 22 million people between the ages of fourteen and sixty-five, out of a total population of 33 million, were in some form of war work. Those who were not in uniform performed vital jobs in factories across the nation.

Women, as we have seen, worked incredibly long shifts to reach their target figures in the production of aircraft, shells, guns, bombs and bullets – work which was depicted graphically in the 1943 semi-documentary-style feature film 'Millions Like Us', starring Patricia Roc.

Music helped morale on the Home Front and the BBC responded with programming specifically aimed at civilians helping the war effort. Although radio had already entered some workshops, the BBC's 'official' 'Music While You Work' programme began broadcasting on 23 June 1940. Initially, the programme transmitted a mixture of non-vocal music played by dance bands, light

ONE OF THE MOST FAMILIAR VOICES OF BBC WARTIME RADIO BROADCASTING BELONGED TO NEWSREADER STUART HIBBERD.

You Must Remember This...

OFF THE BUSES FOR A LUNCHTIME
SINGALONG AS 'LET THE PEOPLE SING'
VISITS THE LONDON PASSENGER
TRANSPORT BOARD.

orchestras and military and brass bands. Popular vocal music was restricted because of the fear that production would fall if the workers listened to sentimental songs or concentrated on their lyrics. It was for this reason that the higher-ups decreed that the programme should have a high content of military and brass-band music (to counter what was perceived as the morale-sapping 'slushy' sentiments of the popular songs). Later, as it became apparent that high morale was not contingent solely on a high quotient of martial music, these programme guidelines were relaxed.

'Music While You Work' was transmitted in two sessions (mid-morning and mid-afternoon) each day, with a third night-time session introduced in August 1942. The programme was a tremendous success: by the end of the war it was being listened to by more than 4.5 million

factory workers and by almost as many people again in workshops, private homes, and forces and Naafi canteens. Not only did the programme provide what its makers claimed was 'an excellent antidote to monotony and boredom', but (and contrary to initial pessimistic expectations) it actually had a beneficial effect on factory output. In its 1945 Yearbook, the BBC quoted one factory report which said: 'The music exhilarates the workers without acting as a harmful distraction. When the [radio] set was shut down for a week there was a 20 per cent drop in output.'

In order to keep the workers happily singing and whistling while they worked, in May 1941 the BBC added a lunchtime variety show, called 'Workers' Playtime', to its long list of wartime radio entertainment. This was a live, twice-weekly broadcast following the 12.30 news bulletin. It differed from other programmes in that each 'Workers' Playtime' was broadcast from a different shop floor. The first was transmitted from a factory in Wexham. The programme was introduced by an England-domiciled Australian radio producer, 'Big' Bill Gates, whose boisterous welcoming to

Worker's Playtime

the show – 'Ladies and Gentlemen: WORKERS' PLAYTIME!' – became as familiar to radio listeners as the news announcers who preceded it. (Breaking with the BBC's pre-war policy, these news readers gave their real names when commencing and closing a bulletin by the Central Office of Information – so that there could be no possibility of the enemy jamming the news and slotting in their own propaganda. Of these wartime announcers, perhaps the best remembered are Alvar Liddell, Stuart Hibberd and Wilfred Pickles (who went on to become a star radio and TV presenter with his own show, 'Have a Go').

The locations of each of these broadcasts were always a secret, and were preceded with the station announcement that it came from a canteen 'somewhere in England'. Although the thirty-minute variety shows were always headlined by a 'name' performer, they were also a fertile nursery for up-and-coming young professionals, and many a future star got his or her first big break on 'Workers' Playtime'. One of the unofficial signature tunes of the show was Noel Gay's hit, *Let the People Sing*, and the factory girls would do full justice to the command, singing their lungs out at the end of the show each in the

AFTER THE WAR, POPULAR WARTIME NEWSREADER WILFRED PICKLES (RIGHT) HAD NEW SUCCESS AS THE PRESENTER OF THE BBC RADIO QUIZ SHOW, 'HAVE A GO'.

Tommy Handley was the radio comedian who made the nation laugh during the dark years of the war and the gloom of austerity that followed. His most famous radio series, 'ITMA' 'It's *That Man Again*', began only days after war was declared in 1939 and continued until his death a decade later. The programme poked gentle fun at the British way of life through its repertoire of characters and situations – Mrs Mopp the cleaner, the Office of Twerps (which took a much-appreciated swipe at the idiocy of government bureaucracy), and the inhabitants of the seaside resort Foaming-at-the-Mouth – which helped cheer the nation. Handley started a style of British humour which was carried on in subsequent generations by the Goons and Monty Python. The ITMA catchphrases included: Mrs Mopp ('Can I do you now, Sir?'), Ali-Oop ('I go – I come back'), Col. Chinstrap ('I don't mind if I do'), and Mona Lott ('It's being so cheerful keeps me going').

The ITMA crew included Tommy Handley, Jack Train, Dorothy Summers, Fred Yule, Hattie Jacques, and Derek Guyler.

(ABOVE): TOMMY HANDLEY (CENTRE) WITH 'NOTORIOUS GERMAN SPY', FUNF (JACK TRAIN, LEFT) AND SIGNOR SO-SO (DINO GALVANI).

vain hope that their voices would be heard above all the others and recognized by family and friends sitting attentively around their radio sets.

> *Let the people sing,*
> *Let the welcome ring,*
> *Anything to kill the 'blues'.*
> *Find a merry song to cheer them*
> *When things all go wrong.*
> *You will find a song,*
> *Welcome as a breath of spring,*
> *Therefore, let the people sing.*

Later, the BBC introduced yet another innovatory programme directed at factory workers, 'Works Wonders'. Here, full rein was given to talents of the workers themselves, who became the stars of the show. Other radio programmes also helped fill the hours and drive the blues away. Vera Lynn had her own radio show, 'Sincerely Yours', beamed to the troops, while that other sweetheart of the forces, Anne Shelton, had two radio shows, 'Calling Malta' and 'Introducing Anne'. Other popular favourites included 'Hi Gang' with ex-pat Americans Ben Lyon and Bebe Daniels, 'Garrison Theatre' (which featured Jack Warner and his famous monologues and 'blue pencil' skits on military censors long before Dock Green beckoned), 'Bandwaggon', and, of course, the most important morale-booster of all – Tommy Handley's ITMA.

Request programmes were extremely popular during the war. Sandy Macpherson presented the first – 'Sandy

Calling' – of what was to become a staple of the radio diet. By 1942 there were more than fifty request programmes on the air. Freddie Grisewood's 'Your Cup of Tea' and Ronnie Shiner's 'Home Town' are two of the best remembered, but Vera Lynn's 'Sincerely Yours', which started in November 1941, was without question the most popular. Requests of a different sort were addressed in Howard Thomas's 'The Brains Trust'.

Factory work generated its own songs as well. As already seen, *Rosie the Riveter* and *The Thing-Ummy-Bob Song* extolled the contribution of women factory workers to the war effort. The comedy song *The Five O'Clock Whistle* struck a chord on both sides of the Atlantic as people worked long hours in the factories

– and frequently needed an excuse to explain why they didn't come home until the early hours of the morning.

> *You oughta hear what my mommy said,*
> *When Poppa came home and sneaked*
>   *into bed,*
> *I told her he worked 'til half past two,*
> *'Cause the 5 o'clock whistle never blew.*

The BBC's output during the war years was not limited to the Home Front, however. A forces programme was started in February 1940 to deliver light entertainment to the troops and differed from previous BBC output in giving the soldiers what they wanted rather than what the BBC thought was 'good' for them. The new programme was broadcast for twelve hours each day, seven days a week (thus breaking one of the BBC's golden rules of the pre-war period: no dance or popular music on Sundays). It proved to be so popular that it was soon attracting not only its targeted military audience but also a huge civilian audience as well. Indeed, listening figures indicated that there were even more civilians listening to the forces programme than tuned in to their own programme, the Home Service. The relaxation of the BBC rules on Sunday music undoubtedly had much to do with this turn of events; the fact that the forces

THOUSANDS DANCED TO TOMMY DORSEY'S GREATEST HIT, *ON THE SUNNY SIDE OF THE STREET.*

The big bands all had their ardent and adoring fans in much the same way that pop and rock stars do today. And the kids collected and swapped records and photographs of the band-leaders, their top side-men (solo instrumentalists) and, to a lesser extent, their vocalists. The repertoire of the British bands was a mix of home-grown music and arrangements copied from such great American bands as those of Benny Goodman, Tommy and Jimmy Dorsey, Artie Shaw, Harry James, Duke Ellington and, of course, Glenn Miller. There are many more references to the immeasurable contribution Major Miller made with his superb orchestra and unique sound in other chapters, but the influence he had on the music scene of the time can only be compared with that of Elvis Presley in the 1950s or the Beatles in the Sixties. Miller, like Presley and the Beatles, stood alone. His band represents the pinnacle of an era. And just as the pop stars of the 1950s and the 1960s became the inspiration of thousands of aspiring musicians of their generation, so it was with the dance bands of the late 1930s and early 1940s which, ranging in

programme also broadcast top singers and bands from America might also have contributed to its success.

It was really the big swing bands of Britain that the young and the young-at-heart wanted to listen to on the air and to dance to in the ballrooms. Gramophone record sales for favourite orchestras and songs from both sides of the Atlantic reached an all-time high. This was the golden age of the big band, an era which reached its zenith in the war years. The best of British bands included: Ambrose, Billy Cotton, Lew Stone, Sidney Lipton, Jack Hylton, Joss Loss (known as 'the British Glenn Miller' because of his signature tune, *In the Mood*), Maurice Winnick, Sid Phillips, and Geraldo. Their wireless slots were eagerly awaited by their fans and were instantly recognized by their distinctive signature tunes which opened and closed the programmes.

You Must Remember This...

90

Worker's Playtime

size from trios to full orchestras, seemed to spring up on every street corner.

As we have seen, the mandarins at the BBC initially limited the broadcast of popular vocal music, be it imported or home-grown because they believed that 'sentimental' songs weakened the spirit. As a result, the BBC sought ways to counter the pernicious influence of such songs. An 'anti-slush' committee was empanelled and made several recommendations. One, which was put into effect in April 1943,, was the requirement that every third song broadcast by the popular dance bands had to be an instrumental – in order to counterbalance the 'slushy' vocals that were reckoned to sap morale. The anti-slush committee also produced a list of singers who were banned from performing on the air. Officially, this was because of their alleged 'incompetence', although many people believed that it was the nature of their lyrics rather than the quality of performance to which the BBC heads objected.

In protecting the morals (and morale) of the nation the BBC banned many songs outright. *Melody Maker* published a list of sixteen banned songs that included *Why Don't We Do This More Often?, That Lovely Weekend,* and *Concerto for Two.* So keen was the BBC to preserve the morals of the nation that certain composers were also banned or heavily censored. Fats Waller's joyous, but ambiguous, lyrics (e.g. 'This is so good it must be illegal') exercised the

GLENN MILLER GETS 'IN THE MOOD' TO SWING.

censors. With even less justification, Johnny Black's First World War song *Paper Doll* was, for a time, discouraged by the authorities, who felt that its lyric about a faithless girl back home might sow the wrong sort of sentiment among soldiers listening in far-off outposts. That the lyric started with the statement 'I guess I've had a million dolls or more', seems to have been lost on its censors.

> *I'm gonna buy a paper doll that I can call my own,*
> *A doll that other fellas cannot steal…*
> *…I'd rather have a paper doll to call my own*
> *Than have a fickle, real-live girl.*

The song *I Heard You Cried Last Night* was similarly banned because it could imply that a soldier was crying. And, of course, Noël Coward fell foul of the censors who, completely missing the irony of his classic *Don't Let's Be Beastly to the Germans*, condemned the song for giving comfort to the enemy.

Despite its ban, *That Lovely Weekend*, written by Ted and Moira Heath, was one of the most popular and enduring songs of the war. It appealed equally to soldiers on leave and to the wives and lovers who were about to say goodbye, as well as to those celebrating more transient affairs. As a result, *That Lovely Weekend* became 'our song' for countless thousands of young couples. Yet, this, one of the most fondly remembered songs of the war, was also banned by many US radio stations – again for fear of corrupting the morals of impressionable young soldiers. (Its lyric does not specify whether the couple in the song are actually married.)

> I haven't said thanks for that lovely
>   weekend,
> Those two days of heaven you helped
>   me to spend,
> The thrill of your kiss as you stepped
>   off the train,
> The smile in your eyes like the sun
>   after rain.
> To mark the occasion we went out to dine,
> Remember the laughter, the music,
>   the wine;

> That drive in the taxi when
> midnight had flown,
> Then breakfast next morning, just we
>   two alone.

That Lovely Weekend was written while Ted Heath was with Geraldo's Orchestra. Heath, a jazz-trombone player living from gig to gig at the time he wrote this 'standard', was, at the end of the war, able to finance from the royalties what became arguably Britain's greatest ever big band – the Ted Heath Orchestra. Certainly, it was regarded by such American jazz giants as Duke Ellington and Count Basie, who often guested in the line-up, as one of the best swing bands on either side of the 'pond'.

Machinations of the anti-slush committee aside, it was songs such as these that the public and the soldiers clamoured for. As a result, there was an enormous production of sentimental and emotional songs on both sides of the Atlantic. And while most of the patriotic and martial music encouraged by the generals and the BBC mandarins have now faded from memory, it is the love songs produced in the war years that have become the evergreen classics of today.

CHAPTER TEN

The American Invaders

Got Any Gum, Chum?

ON 7 DECEMBER 1941 the war entered a new phase. The long delay by the Americans in entering what they perceived to be a European war was brought abruptly to an end by the Japanese sneak attack on the US naval base at Pearl Harbor, Hawaii. In one stroke the inherent neutrality and isolationism of the American people was shattered. And when the Americans finally did enter the war they did so with determination.

The shock of Pearl Harbor brought its own call to arms. Composer Frank Loesser put to music the story of the ship's chaplain who leapt to man the anti-aircraft guns after his shipmates had been killed in the attack. The song's title,

IT'S BOOGIE-WOOGIE TIME INSIDE RAINBOW CORNER, THE LONDON CLUB FOR AMERICAN SERVICEMEN.

Praise the Lord and Pass the Ammunition, incorporated the chaplain's words, and became the battle cry of the nation. It had enormous popularity in Britain as well, where it was recorded by Joe Loss and His Orchestra.

> *Praise the Lord and pass the ammunition,*
> *And we'll all stay free.*
> *Praise the Lord and swing into position,*
> *Can't afford to be a politician.*
> *Praise the Lord, we're all between*
>   *perdition,*
> *And the deep blue sea.*
> *Yes, the sky pilot said it,*
> *You've got to give him credit,*
> *For a son of a gunner was he,*
> *Shouting 'Praise the Lord, we're on a*
>   *mighty mission,*
> *All aboard, we're not a-goin' fishin','*
> *Praise the Lord and pass the ammunition,*
> *And we'll all stay Free – Free.*

After the war, Loesser's career as a song-writer went from strength to strength, culminating in what many regard as the greatest stage musical of them all – 'Guys and Dolls'.

After the Japanese attack on Pearl Harbor, American songwriters unleashed a wave of jingoistic invective against the enemy. While their lyrics may not have withstood the test of time, they accurately reflect the mood of the period. Songs such as Ralph Stockton and Junie Cobb's *He'll Put An Ax to the Axis* and Frank Kraushaar and Orell Hibbard's *Headin' for Berlin* were typical of the first frantic jingoistic outpourings.

> *Oh, Tokio be patient,*
> *We just hate to be rushed,*
> *'Cause first there's little Adolf,*
> *Who has to hear from us.*

Bob Miller's *We're Gonna Have to Slap That Dirty Little Jap* was just one of the many explicit songs that followed the American entry into the war. Leaving no room for doubt, the song proclaimed:

> *We'll murder Hirohito,*
> *Massacre that slob Benito,*
> *Hang 'em with that Shicklegrüber,*

before concluding that:

> *Uncle Sam's the guy who can do it!*

(The reference to Hitler as Shicklegrüber was a common feature of songs of that time. Many songs of the period cast aspersions on Hitler's parentage. These ranged from the banned *Even Hitler Had a Mother* to *Old Man Schicklegrüber*.)

The first Yanks arrived in Britain barely a month after the Japanese attack brought America into the war. The first American troopships landed in Belfast in January 1942. Recognizing the troops' arrival in Ireland but also with an eye to the large Irish minority in America, *Johnny Doughboy Found a Rose in Ireland*, by American songwriters Al Goodhart and Kay Twomey, stressed the common roots of the Allies. With its reference to Johnny Doughboy's mother in old New York, who 'spoke the sweetest blarney

The American Invaders

AN AMERICAN GI SHOWS A BRITISH
SCHOOLBOY THE AUTHENTIC WAY TO DUNK A
DOUGHNUT.

too', the song appealed to the common
links joining the two peoples. The last
verse predicted a rosy future for Johnny
and the Irish rose who had stolen his
heart:

> He said 'Darlin' 'tis my duty
> To make an American beauty
> Of a sweet Irish rose like you.'

('American Beauty' is the name of a
popular rose grown in the United States.)

The arrival of American servicemen in Britain – by the war's end some
3.5 million American soldiers passed
through Britain – was not without incident. Some observers, like F.E. Huggett,
commented favourably on them. 'The
American invasion struck the British Isles
like a huge Technicolor bomb, scattering
nylons, cigarettes and candy and goodwill
over the whole country.' But in other
quarters the Americans met with hostility.
As George Orwell reported a year into
the American invasion, there was an initial
antipathy between American servicemen
and their British hosts. According to
Orwell there was a 'widespread anti-
American feeling among the working
class thanks to the presence of the
American soldiers, and, I believe, very
bitter anti-British feeling among the
soldiers themselves.' It was a classic case

of culture clash. The
Americans found Britain dingy, old-
fashioned, class-ridden and poverty-riven,
while the British found the Americans
brash and boastful, resented both their
high level of pay and the fact that valuable
shipping was taken up in transporting
'luxury' foods and goods to the GIs. It
hurt all the more that these same goods
were denied to their own children either
because they were rationed – chocolates,
sweets, fruit – or, as in the case of ice
cream, altogether prohibited. Most
importantly, they resented the Americans'
sexual activities. The threefold complaint
that the Americans were 'overpaid, oversexed, and over here' was common.

The potential for a falling out
among the Allies was great and several
measures were taken to alleviate the
tensions. Margaret Mead, the eminent
American anthropologist who had made
her reputation with her famous book on
the sexual activities of Samoan teenagers
(*Coming of Age in Samoa*), was despatched

to Britain to research the culture clash first hand. Her report, published in pamphlet form, was distributed to American troops stationed in Britain in the hope that knowledge of British mores might help keep them out of trouble.

The British government turned to the cinema to explain British customs and society to the Americans. In 1943 the Ministry of Information produced an hour-long film, 'A Welcome to Britain', which was given to the American Office of War Information to show to its troops. With wit and humour the Americans were introduced to the etiquette of the pub, the intricacies of British currency, the geography of Britain, the extent and effects of rationing, and even given advice on how best to deal with the 'working girls' of Soho ('watch your step'). The film, which included sequences featuring Burgess Meredith and Bob Hope was a rousing success both with the troops and with the critics – although, like Margaret Mead's handy pamphlet, it was never shown to the British public.

As seen in the next chapter, the commercial cinema also helped smooth relations between the two cultures. In 1941 Twentieth Century Fox sent Tyrone Power to be 'A Yank in the RAF' in an early attempt to help bridge the gap between Britain and America. A year later, MGM sent spoiled rich kid Mickey Rooney (at that time the most popular actor in America) to be arguably the most unlikely 'Yank at Eton'. Scarcely

more credible was Rita Hayworth as a Windmill Theatre showgirl in Columbia's 1945 'Tonight and Every Night'. Yet pictures such as these and the many others of the same genre, both American – 'Pimpernel Smith' (1941), 'Mrs Miniver' (1942), 'Flying Fortress' (1942), 'San Demetrio London' (1943) – and British – 'The Foreman Went to France' (1942), 'The Way to the Stars' (1945) – helped break down the barriers between the two cultures. So, too, did the songs that bridged the cultural gap. The all-American tribute *Ma, I Miss Your Apple Pie* was popular on both sides of the Atlantic, precisely because it expressed the feelings of all soldiers far from home.

Oh Ma, I miss your apple pie,
Ma, I miss your stew.
Ma, they're treating me alright,
But they can't cook like you.

That the Americans were overpaid, at least by British standards, cannot be denied. American service personnel were paid five times as much as their British counterparts. Thus, the wages of an enlisted man in the US army, much to the chagrin of some people, were as high as those of a British officer. Additionally, the GIs had access to the PX ('Post Exchange'), where almost every sort of luxury good was available. Virtual Aladdin's caves of goodies, the PXs contained many items that had not been seen in Britain for years – chewing gum, sweets, oranges, plentiful butter, spirits.

The American Invaders

THE LAST TIME THE BRITISH SET OFF TO THE AMERICAS ON SUCH AN EXCITING ADVENTURE WAS WHEN THE PILGRIM FATHERS SAILED ON THE *MAYFLOWER*. THESE GI BRIDES ARE ABOUT TO SET SAIL ON THE *QUEEN MARY*, IN 1946.

Americans', their generosity usually smoothed over what could have become a major problem. British airmen lucky enough to be diverted to American air bases because of adverse weather revelled in the riches made available to them. Many British homes also benefited, and proudly displayed cartons of Camels or Lucky Strikes and tins of peaches in the larder provided visible testimony of the generosity of American friends. This generosity was celebrated in such songs as *Thanks, Mr Roosevelt* and the more overt *Got Any Gum, Chum?*

But nothing strained the relations between the two allies more than their respective attitudes towards sexual behaviour. The room for misunderstanding was great and proved a constant irritant, at least for some people. While popular with British women (because they were generous, kind, and confident), the GIs had an altogether different effect on British men – particularly those who were posted far away from their families.

There were many opportunities for fraternization between American servicemen and British women. On the Home Front it was still business as usual

Additionally, they held huge quantities of items that were either rationed or in short supply in Britain. Cigarettes were so cheap in the PX that GIs bought them by the carton – an unheard-of luxury at a time when many Britons bought them individually. Soap, which was rationed, and almost equally hard-to-come-by razor-blades were easily obtainable by Americans in their PXs; while ice cream, which had been banned for the duration in September 1942, was available only on American bases. As the war dragged on it seemed as if Americans not only bagged all the taxis, but they were the only ones to have access to petrol. Perhaps most precious of all, however, were the newly invented nylon stockings, which no British girl had ever seen before. Although the GIs' easy access to these and other goods sometimes added to the local resentment against the 'invading

in theatres, cinemas and, of course, dance halls, where many of the customers not only danced to American swing music, but also now had US servicemen to show them how to do the jitterbug properly. The GIs found partners as easy to come by as falling leaves in autumn, much to the annoyance of British servicemen, and many a western saloon barroom-style brawl broke out between the 'Allies' in the dance halls and pubs of Britain, mostly over the affection of girls. The Yanks not only had a relaxed, Hollywood movieland image in the eyes of susceptible young women, but also seemed to have comparatively large amounts of money, being able to ply them with all sorts of luxuries. And while the incidence of sexually transmitted diseases soared during the war years (as did the number of illegitimate births), not all liaisons were illicit. Over 70,000 British women became GI brides, leaving home after the war to start a new life in the USA.

The claim that the American soldiers were 'oversexed' may be misdirected. Sexual activity was certainly heightened during the war, but there is little evidence – at least through the lyrics of their songs – that the Americans were any more highly sexed than their British counterparts. Songs like Ted and Moira Heath's *That Lovely Weekend* and Eric Maschwitz and George Posford's *Room Five Hundred and Four* were, after all, written by British songwriters for the British audience.

Such a big hotel, a very grand one,
Right up the avenue.
We could not afford it,
But, Sweet, I just adored it,
My very first and only rendezvous.

The lovely night,
The starlight above,
The sleeping town below;
And in the dark you said, my love,
The dearest things I know.

Such songs do, of course, also provide evidence that illicit and casual sex were not far below the surface of people's thoughts, if not their behaviour. Psychologists have commented on the heightened sexual activity that takes place in war zones where, for many people, the drive to live for today is strong because of the uncertainty that there will ever be a tomorrow.

Many songs of the period deal with sexual subjects either overtly or by implication. There are myriad songs that provide instructions, admonitions, protestations, or pleas. *Lady be Good, Ain't Misbehavin', Faithful Forever, I Shall be Waiting, I'll Never Smile Again, I'll Walk Alone, It's Always You, Why Don't We Do This More Often?, I Don't Want to Walk Without You, I Got it Bad and That Ain't Good, Keep an Eye on Your Heart, One More Kiss, I Wanna Get Married, I Hope to Die If I Told a Lie,* and countless more expressed the hopes and fears of couples thrown together or torn apart by the war.

Many encapsulated chat-up lines and the emotional blackmail used at the time. *You Can't Say 'No' to a Soldier* (with its immortal line 'If he's gonna fight he's got a right to romance') was a typically lighthearted example of the genre.

More serious was Bobby Worth's *A Fellow on a Furlough* (GI-speak for leave), which talks about the loneliness of a soldier on leave far from home and the transient thrills in his search for company:

Oh pretty lady, you'll hear him say,
Beautiful lady, are you going my way?
He's just a fellow on a furlough,
Whose hopes have all come true.

Manning Sherwin and Tommy Connor's *Who's Taking You Home Tonight?* was a favourite last waltz at dances. Often it was sung (or whispered) by couples as they danced, giving impetus to many a tryst. The song's hopeful lyrics had special meaning for the many young servicemen who did not know if they would survive the war, and the many women who could never know whether this night might be the last with their loved one.

Who's taking you home tonight?
Darling, it's plain to see,
I'm pleading,
Please let it be me.

But for every come-on there was another song that prescribed good behaviour. Perhaps the most famous of all was the Andrews Sisters' recording of *Don't Sit*

Under the Apple Tree (With Anyone Else But Me). This enormously popular song had both a great tune and a swinging rhythm. But most important of all was the highly appropriate lyric that summed up the feelings of many couples separated by the war. The song's serious message is told in a humorous way as it alternates promises of fidelity by the girl and instructions to her partner (and threats of the consequences if he steps out of line) while they're apart, to conclude:

Be fair to me and I'll guarantee
This is one thing I will do.
I won't sit under the apple tree with
*   anyone else but you,*
'Til you come marching home.

The song obviously expressed a universal feeling. That it appeared in no fewer than

three wartime films ('Buck Privates', 'Private Buckaroo', and 'With a Song in My Heart') could only have accelerated its rocketing popularity.

Even seemingly innocuous songs had a certain sexual content in some contexts. *You are My Sunshine*, written by Jimmy Davis and Charles Mitchell, carried what might well be a subliminal message to the troops. Easy to sing with a cheery chorus, it was a popular singalong song. Although it is its chorus that first comes to mind, the lyric had other resonances as well.

> *The other night, dear, as I lay dreaming,*
> *I dreamt that you were by my side.*
> *Came disillusion when I awoke, dear,*
> *You were gone and then I cried.*

The most famous meeting place in London, and the target of every GI on a twenty-four-hour pass, was Rainbow Corner. Located on Piccadilly, this club run by the American Red Cross was a haven for GIs and the British girls who wanted to meet them. It was the site of innocent pleasure where many genuine friendships and romantic liaisons began, although the area around it was notorious for attracting another sort of encounter altogether. On the edge of Soho, the area teemed with prostitutes. In blackout conditions they flashed the beams of their torches on their ankles as a sign that their whispered 'Hiya, Joe' was more than a simple greeting.

It is a popular fallacy that the American troops brought the new form of dancing – jitterbugging – to Britain. In fact, the dance craze had appeared on the scene well before the first American troops arrived. The first national jitterbug championship was held during the Phoney War period, in February 1940, at the Paramount Ballroom in London, two full years before American GIs reached Britain's shores. Indeed, as we have seen, by 1940 doing the jitterbug was so popular that many fainthearted ballroom owners actually banned it in order to protect their precious sprung floors.

The arrival of the Americans did, however, shift the dance into a new gear. No longer was it a minority interest. GIs and their British dance partners helped transform the jitterbug from cult interest to general fashion. In the process, they changed the whole nature of the dance-hall phenomenon. Where formerly there had been a graceful, circular movement of dancers around the floor, now there were the wild gyrations of hip cats who pecked, trucked, leapt and dived.

Of course, American music in general had reached Britain long before the outbreak of war. But it only became really popular with the arrival of American troops. Although there was some British interest in jazz in the 1920s, this was primarily a cult interest. In the 1930s some of the great jazz musicians – Louis Armstrong, Duke Ellington, Cab Calloway – toured Britain, but the protectionism of the musicians' unions in

both countries inhibited the free flow of musical talent. But with the troops came their music. Within a short time it was not only the American bases that swung to the new music, but also the ballrooms and dance halls up and down the country.

It was big band music that made the most distinctive impact. Even prior to the Yanks' arrival, wartime dance halls had been filled with the signature tunes of the most famous of the big bands. Woody Herman's *Woodchoppers' Ball*, Artie Shaw's *Night and Day*, and Glenn Miller's *Moonlight Serenade* were all being belted out not only by American musicians, but also by their British colleagues (*In the Mood*, for example, was also Joe Loss's signature tune and *Bugle Call Rag* was Harry Roy's). But songs with an even more American flavour entered the British repertoire – *Ma I Miss Your Apple Pie, Deep in the Heart of Texas, Chattanooga Choo Choo, Pennsylvania 6–5000, I've Got a Gal in Kalamazoo,* and *American Patrol* (with its swinging version of nineteenth-century John Philip Sousa marches).

Glenn Miller and his AAF Orchestra arrived in Britain shortly after D–Day with a brief to entertain the troops. This they did through numerous

You Must Remember This...

THE GLENN MILLER ORCHESTRA AT TOP SPEED ON THE *CHATTANOOGA CHOO-CHOO*, WHICH EARNED THE WORLD'S FIRST GOLD DISC.

personal appearances at bases and hospitals around the country – often with two or even three shows a day – as well as through Miller's own radio programmes on the American Forces Network. The latter were beamed directly toward the bases from low-power transmitters, so civilians in the vicinity were also able to pick up these broadcasts on their radio sets and many became keen listeners. Miller also broadcast on the main BBC stations. The Miller Band brought with them a huge number of songs whose simple, unencumbered lyrics delighted listeners everywhere.

> *ABCDEFGH I got a gal*
> *In Kalamazoo,*
> *I don't want to boast, but I know she's*
>   *the toast*
> *Of Kalamazoo.*

But if any song captured the spirit of the time it was one that appeared in the Glenn Miller film 'Orchestra Wives'. Written in 1932 by Jack Sherr and Gonzalo Roig, its lyric assumed even greater poignancy for lovers separated by the war. *Yours* was one of the biggest hits of the war and became 'our song' for countless thousands of wartime lovers:

> *Yours 'til the stars lose their glory!*
> *Yours 'til the birds fail to sing!*
> *Yours to the end of life's story,*
> *This pledge to you dear I bring!*

Although he was in Britain for only six months, Glenn Miller had an enormous influence on the nation's wartime music. In many ways, the Glenn Miller experience can be seen as a microcosm of the Americans' impact on Britain. The short, sharp shock that both occasioned is still reverberating fifty years later.

CHAPTER ELEVEN

Showbiz at War

Hooray for Hollywood, Three Cheers for Borehamwood

MOVIES WERE IMPORTANT BOTH at home and in the field. Mobile cinemas showed films to the soldiers stationed overseas, bringing them, even if only for a few hours, a bit of home.

LAURENCE OLIVIER IN HIS FAMOUS FILM VERSION OF SHAKESPEARE'S 'HENRY V'.

The cinema was enormously popular during the war. Never had so many people gone to see films. Between 25 and 30 million seats were sold each week! Escapist fare was the film-goer's favourite and the production of musicals, westerns, South Sea-island romances and the like soared during the war years. Cinema also proved to be a marvellous means of communicating wartime information to its huge audiences. Several different sorts of film were employed for this, including the many 'information' trailers about rationing and recipes, newsreels and official government Ministry of Information bulletins. Singalong musical shorts were a popular part of the daily programme.

Feature films from both sides of the Atlantic were important in to helping maintain morale. This was done in several ways. There were glorious flag-wavers

THE FILM CLASSIC, 'SINCE YOU WENT AWAY'.

like Laurence Olivier's 'Henry V', comedies like 'Let George Do it', and the pure escapism of such westerns as 'Destry Rides Again' and South-Seas epics like 'Song of the Islands'. But morale-boosters of a more subtle variety were also produced. Two of the greatest classics came from Hollywood – 'Mrs Miniver' and 'Since You Went Away'. Both these films portrayed ordinary people getting on with their lives in the extraordinary circumstances of the war. It has been argued that these films were second only to the Japanese attack on Pearl Harbor in swaying American public opinion towards war.

The film successes of the early months of hostilities were 'Goodbye, Mr Chips', starring Robert Donat, who won an Oscar for his role; 'Jamaica Inn', with Charles Laughton; 'Where's That Fire?' with comedian Will Hay; and 'Come On, George', starring George Formby. Significantly, none of the storylines of these pictures touched even remotely on the impending conflict: they were escapism pure and simple from the fear and uncertainties of the unfolding real-life world drama.

As the war progressed, the cinemas took on an even greater importance in many people's lives. Cinemas were places of both mental and physical comfort. They were the one escape from the unrelenting grind and privations.

Architecturally, the great cinemas were palaces of almost Oriental pleasure – Alhambras and Odeons where, for a short time at least, it was the imagination and not the world that ran riot. And it is not entirely coincidental that at a time when fuel was short, they were one of the few places that could be relied upon to be comfortably warm.

Although cinemas were closed early in the blitz for fear of bombs, their importance for morale was quickly realized and they were soon reopened – albeit with restricted hours. (For a time, cinemas shut at 6pm to enable their patrons to get home before the blackout and the blitz made travel too hazardous.) Yet cinema owners had never had it so good. The queues for cinema tickets were huge, often stretching around the block even – or, given the comfort they offered, perhaps especially – in the most inclement weather.

The war years were a golden age for British cinema in another way as well. Not only did people throng to the cinemas in their millions, but some of the finest British films of all time – Olivier's 'Henry V', Coward's 'In Which We Serve' and Powell and Pressberger's 'The Life and Death of Colonel Blimp' – were produced during these turbulent years.

These three films all had to overcome obstacles when they were first made. The government initially censored 'Colonel Blimp' on the grounds that it expressed ambiguity towards the Germans and showed the British officer class in a bad light. Similarly, the Ministry of Information opposed the Noël Coward film 'In Which We Serve' (which portrayed the sinking of a British destroyer and its crew's efforts to survive in a life-dinghy) because, it said, it was bad propaganda. It took an appeal by Louis Mountbatten (the film was based on events from his life) to his cousin the King to achieve the release of what has since become recognized as one of the finest British war movies ever made.

'In Which We Serve' won Noël Coward an Academy Award nomination for best writer and introduced to the screen Richard (now Lord) Attenborough. Paying homage to the armed services, it also set a standard for other feature films – indeed, some of the pictures it inspired rose almost to Coward's heights. If 'In Which We Serve' showed the real spirit of the Royal Navy in times of war, then 'The Way Ahead' had a similar impact on behalf of the army. This film, written by Eric Ambler and Peter Ustinov and starring David Niven and Stanley Holloway, followed a platoon of raw recruits through training and battle.

'Henry V', released shortly after D-Day in 1944, was also subject to initial criticism, albeit this time from the press and the public rather than the government. Olivier, who was released from his RAF duties to make the film, suffered extremely bad publicity because it was

You Must Remember This...

(LEFT): 'GLAD YOU'RE OVER HERE', SAID THE SNOWDROP (MILITARY POLICEMAN) TO ACTOR JAMES CAGNEY. *(BELOW):* FRANK SINATRA WITH GENE KELLY AS A COUPLE OF GIRL-HUNGRY SAILORS ON LEAVE IN NEW YORK IN THE MGM MUSICAL, 'ON THE TOWN'.

shot in (neutral) Ireland. Moreover, the film chewed up a huge amount of resources as, at the time of its release, it was the most expensive British picture ever made. Its clear allegory to current events – deftly pointed out in the 'dedication' to those who led the D-Day attack – and the rousing patriotic sentiment it engendered more than compensated for the initial derision. Today 'Henry V' is recognized as a classic of British cinema.

Of course, not all British films resorted to allegory to get their message across. Many showed in no uncertain terms just how tough and resolute the armed services could be. 'In Which We Serve' was the first real 'stiff-upper-lipper'. Made in 1942, it starred Noël Coward – who also produced, wrote, composed the score and partially directed the film (the other part was directed by a promising newcomer named David Lean who went on to make 'Brief Encounter', 'Lawrence of Arabia' and 'The Bridge On the River Kwai').

Arguably the best of the many films about the Royal Air Force was the memorable comedy-drama 'The Way to the Stars'. Although made in 1945, it was based on the RAF experiences of its creator, playwright Terence Rattigan, during

DANNY KAYE – WHOSE TRUIMPHS AT THE LONDON PALLADIUM HAVE NEVER BEEN SURPASSED – PERFORMS *MINNIE THE MOOCHER* WITH THE SKYROCKETS.

the Battle of Britain in 1941. It had a musical score by Nicholas Brodsky which still has the power to bring a tear to the eye more than fifty years after it was written. The film concludes with *Johnny in the Clouds,* the evocatively atmospheric poem by John Pudney (which was used as the title for its American release).

> *Fetch out no shroud,*
> *For Johnny in the cloud,*
> *And keep your tears,*
> *For him in after years.*
> *Better by far,*
> *For Johnny the bright star,*
> *To keep your head,*
> *And see his children fed.*

Hollywood, too, contributed to the war effort and its well-oiled publicity machine ensured maximum coverage for the big

stars who had enlisted in the armed services. Newspapers and newsreels on both sides of the Atlantic carried pictures of the 'King of Hollywood', Clark Gable, in uniform after he joined up in the air force. Almost as many others showed Col. James Stewart smiling, but with a determined hero-type glint in his eye. (Nine years after the war had ended, Stewart had his greatest ever box-office success playing the title role in 'The Glenn Miller Story'.) Other big names also joined the queue to enlist in the armed services; they came not just from the silver screen, but from stage and radio as well. There is no doubt that the sight of these stars enlisting to fight for Uncle Sam was a tremendous morale-booster for ordinary GIs and civilians alike: if rich movie stars were prepared to risk their necks by joining up then maybe this was a war really worth fighting.

Of course it was not only the stars but also Hollywood itself that geared up for the big fight. Soon after the declaration of war, the movie industry began to

classic stage routines including the number written for him by his wife, Sylvia Fine, *Melody in 4F*. This song, about a hypochondriacal draftee who tries to convince the medical examiners at his draft board that he is 4F (military terminology for 'unfit for military service'), was sung in meaningless scat singing that nevertheless somehow made complete sense. Kaye's co-star, Dinah Shore, also made a great impact by helping Harold Arlen and Ted Kueler win an Oscar with her honey-voiced rendition of their song, *Now I Know*. Shore, who was the American equivalent of Vera Lynn, appeared in several wartime musicals including 'Thank Your Lucky Stars' and 'Follow the Boys' and had many other hit songs, among them the Oscar-nominated *I'll Walk Alone*.

> They call, no date;
> I promised you I'd wait,
> I want them all to know
> I'm strictly single-o.

go into factory-line production with a whole string of patriotic call-to-arms dramas and musicals. One of the most off-beat was 'Up in Arms', which launched the feature film career of Danny Kaye. The critic of the *New York Daily Mirror* wrote of Danny's debut: 'Not since Greta Garbo made her bow has there been anything so terrific as the inimitable Danny, one of the most exhilarating and spontaneous personalities in film history.' In the film, Kaye performed some of his

Britain, having entered the war more than two years earlier than the USA,

already had a long list of star recruits in uniform, including Laurence Olivier, serving as a pilot in the Fleet Air Arm, Michael Redgrave in the Royal Navy, and John Mills in the army. David Niven, who had been a regular British army officer before becoming a Hollywood movie idol, returned to Britain at the outbreak of the war and saw service as a commando officer before taking up staff work at the War Office (where, among other duties, he provided liaison between the BBC and American recording artists).

The propaganda value of getting cinema stars into uniform was enormous, and the role models they provided for countless impressionable young men cannot be denied. However, stars in uniform caused almost as many problems as they solved. Both the Americans and the British found it hard to maintain discipline when there were top stars in their midst. Clark Gable found it impossible to function while based in the United States as his outfit was constantly besieged by his many fans.

An even greater worry was the involvement of stars in combat. Recognizing the huge potential for demoralization should a star die in battle, many were removed (often against their wishes) from battle zones. Nevertheless, many artistes did, in fact, become involved in combat and there were certainly several casualties in the acting profession. One of the most famous was the British international movie star Leslie Howard, who returned to fight for his country shortly after filming 'Gone With the Wind'. After making the films '49th Parallel', 'Pimpernel Smith', 'The First of the Few' (a homage to the Spitfire) and producing 'The Gentle Sex' (about seven female conscripts to the ATS) – all important contributions to the war effort – Howard was sent to Spain and Portugal on behalf of the British government. He never returned. His plane was shot down by a lone German fighter. It was said that the German intelligence services had got wind that there was a VIP on board and believed it to be Winston Churchill. Thereafter, the government decided that a good number of British showbiz names would be more useful in front of a movie camera, or treading the boards again, than flying a plane or firing a gun. So, in spite of their patriotic fervour, some of the biggest stage and screen stars served their time as greasepaint warriors.

One of the most bizarre stories of the Second World War concerning a member of the theatrical profession involved Clifton James, a smalltime provincial repertory actor. James was serving in the Royal Army Pay Corps when he was asked by British intelligence to participate in a deception that was to change his life forever, and give him his first and only starring role. It occurred when Operation Overlord – The D-Day landing – was being secretly planned. British intelligence believed that it would give the Allies tremendous advantage if

You Must Remember This...

the Germans could be fooled into thinking that they knew where the landings were to take place. The idea, therefore, was to convince them that the Allied assault on Europe would commence in southern France. The plan was almost childishly simple. An actor would impersonate General Montgomery, the great hero of the desert campaign, and this 'Monty look-alike' would be seen in the war zones that would seem to confirm that the Allied invasion would indeed be spearheaded in southern France.

Although Clifton James did bear a physical resemblance to Montgomery, he had to study every gesture and move of the great General, even to acquire the idiosyncratic way of speaking in a high-pitched voice with a lisp that pronounced Rs as Ws. Clifton James would rehearse

for days, watching Montgomery on newsreel, and listening to recordings of his voice. At last he was ready for his big dress rehearsal. This was to be a full-scale inspection of British soldiers in Gibraltar, followed by a typical Monty rallying speech of the 'awright men, let's get at them' variety. Clifton James carried out the Monty impersonation faultlessly, and everyone present (including, presumably, German intelligence sources) were convinced that his speech strongly indicated where the Allied attack would be. How successful Clifton James' 'starring role' had been is best summed up, perhaps, by General Sir Leslie Hollis, who said in a public address after the war: 'By this and other methods 450,000 German troops were kept pinned down in various parts of Europe even after the Normandy landings. And the German troops in the south of France were not withdrawn and sent north for ten days following this landing. Had they been available earlier, then the invasion of northern France would have been infinitely more difficult, and the casualties greater.'

After the war, Clifton James recreated his Montgomery impersonation with a tour of British music halls and variety theatres in an act he called 'I Was Monty's Double'. A feature film was made about this incredible Second-World-War confidence trick, using that same stage act title, and giving Clifton James the opportunity to star alongside such cinema luminaries as John Mills, Cecil Parker and Marius Goring.

Impersonation of a different sort was used by the BBC, which sometimes employed actors to record for the nation speeches made earlier in the day by Winston Churchill in Parliament.

Churchill was a keen cinema-goer. His own love affair with the cinema began with an abiding admiration for the Marx Brothers' films, which he reportedly screened in a private cinema within the Cabinet War Rooms whenever he needed a good laugh. Churchill also had a life-long friendship with Hungarian-born British movie mogul Alexander Korda. His association with Korda started just before the war when the impecunious Churchill had gone to the film maker with a script he had written about his illustrious ancestor, the Duke of Marlborough. Korda read Churchill's work and promptly paid him £10,000 for the screen rights in the property – an immense sum for such a transaction in those days. In the event, the film was never made, but it established a bond between the two men which was to pay handsome dividends in the war years. Churchill felt he could really trust Korda and enrolled him in his own private intel-ligence-gathering network, made up mostly of highly-placed businessmen with international connections. Later on in the war, Korda was made an unofficial MI5 agent whilst he was working in Hollywood, where he was in a position to feed back to Churchill the mood of the people in the USA regarding Hitler, and to talk to film makers who, like himself, had the ear of President Roosevelt.

Korda's association with Churchill was not limited to intelligence-gathering. Churchill also wanted Korda to make patriotic British films. Korda responded with the all-star documentary feature 'The Lion has Wings' about the hidden might of the Royal Air Force. The movie hardly broke box-office records, either in Britain or the States, but it nearly broke Korda, whose own fortunes were always teetering on the verge of bankruptcy. As a result, Churchill proposed a much more commercial film to Korda that would not only put 'bums on seats', but would particularly appeal to the then still neutral Americans. It was to be the story of the love between Lord Nelson and Lady Hamilton. In Britain it was called 'Lady Hamilton' and in the States, where it was produced in less than six weeks, 'That Hamilton Woman'. The film starred Laurence Olivier and Vivien Leigh, whom Korda had first introduced to each other, and who had almost immediately become lovers – (they were both married to other partners at the time). It was directed by Korda himself. His excursion behind the camera was a rare occurrence, since he had become the boss of Britain's

THE GREAT BRITISH FILM
COMEDIAN WILL HAY, ON THE
SET OF 'THE GOOSE STEPS OUT'
WITH JOAN ENGLAND, ONE OF
THE FIRST WOMEN FILM
TECHNICIANS.

biggest studio at Denham, the head-quarters of his company, London Films.

'Lady Hamilton' has since been regarded as Korda's most completely satisfying film, even ahead of his Oscar-winning 'The Private Lives of Henry VIII' and it was very strongly rumoured that Churchill's creative contribution is most likely to have been in the scene in which Nelson (brilliantly played by Olivier) pleads with the Lords of the Admiralty not to trust Bonaparte's offer of peace. The analogy with Hitler was plain for all to see. 'Napoleon can never be master of the world until he has smashed us up – and believe me, gentlemen, he means to master the world. You cannot make peace with dictators, you have to destroy them.' This message was clearly lost on Joseph Stalin when Churchill brought the Russian leader a print of the film and gave it to him personally; nevertheless Stalin still managed to make 'Lady Hamilton' the first ever non-Soviet film to get full interstate general release. The only other British films at that time to achieve this status were all those made by George Formby who, particularly in Moscow, became a big favourite.

But it was in the British cinemas – which were breaking records everywhere – that the British film industry really came into its own with home-grown films often outgrossing Hollywood imports. Although there were splendid wartime dramas like Emeric Pressburger and Michael Powell's '49th Parallel' (commissioned by the Ministry of Information to help sway public opinion for America's entry into the war, and for which Pressburger won an Oscar for best screenplay), it was really comedy and

(RIGHT): THE ANDREWS SISTERS IN FOUR-PART HARMONY WITH BING CROSBY.

(BELOW): BOB HOPE (RIGHT) WITH JERRY COLONNA AND THE REST OF HIS TROUPE ON AN EIGHT-WEEK USO TOUR OF EUROPE. THE WEARING OF UNIFORMS BY USO AND ENSA PERFORMERS WAS ESSENTIAL SHOULD THEY BE CAPTURED BY THE ENEMY.

No entertainer put in more air miles than British-born comedian Bob Hope. There was barely a war zone that he and his troupe of entertainers, which often included Dorothy Lamour and Marilyn Maxwell, did not play. Many of the GIs, thousands of miles from home, remember with gratitude how he brought laughter to their bases in far-off places, and are instantly transported back to these times whenever they hear Hope's signature tune, *Thanks for the Memory.*

> *Thanks for the memory,*
> *Of candlelight and wine, and castles*
> *on the Rhine,*
> *The Parthenon, that moment on*
> *the Hudson River Line,*
> *How lovely it was.*

Of course, Hope rewrote the lyric of his theme song for his USO performance:

> *Thanks for the memory,*
> *You Uncle Sammy's crew, our minutes*
> *are too few.*
> *I wish that I could kiss*
> *Each and every one of you.*

As well as gramophone records, ENSA and the American USO – the two largest entertainment agencies in history – poured thousands of entertainers into the field. Between them they employed around 10,000 entertainers who performed for the enjoyment of the troops. In the course of the war the USO employed 5,424 entertainers (of whom 1,522, in 119 units, travelled overseas to entertain the troops). Their effect on the morale of the servicemen cannot be overestimated: by the war's end they had performed before a combined total audience of 172 million.

music that people mainly went to see. They just wanted to forget their troubles for a couple of hours, and the cinema was the place to do it. Sometimes the comedies had a vague wartime connection. Ealing Studios, in particular, turned out a prodigious number of comedies with the Crazy Gang fighting their own fantasy war against Fritz in 'Gas Bags' and Will Hay with his assorted team of 'odd balls' with funny spoofs, including 'The Black Sheep of Whitehall', 'The Ghost of St Michael's' and his anti-Nazi send-up 'The Goose Steps Out'. Meanwhile, that other top comedian Tommy Trinder was giving the Jerries hell in such frolics as 'The Foreman Went to France'.

But it was George Formby who was the number one British draw. His films rang the ticket tills more consistently than those of any other comedy actor with winners like 'Let George Do it', 'Spare a Copper', and 'Turned Out Nice Again', while his gramophone records sold in tens of thousands. Soon to rival him, however, were the American comic double act who made their feature film debut in 1941 with 'Buck Privates' (it was released in Britain, as yet unfamiliar with American military terminology, under the title 'Rookies'). Britain and America were, until the war brought a whole new vocabulary across the Atlantic, still two nations divided by a common language. 'Rookies' launched Abbott and Costello on an international film career that was to last almost ten years, an amazingly long

run for comedians, even today. The film also featured the Andrews Sisters, whose rendition of *The Boogie Woogie Bugle Boy of Company 'B'* won an Academy Award nomination for its writers, Hugh Prince and Don Raye. The song proved to be very popular and featured in several wartime films, becoming a huge hit on both sides of the Atlantic.

And the company jumped
When he played reveille,
He's the boogie woogie bugle boy
of Company 'B'.

In days when gramophone records were scarce, films were a major source of popular songs. This was especially true of American songs – not surprisingly in view of the fact that the war years were also the golden age of the Hollywood musical. Usually, the songs from the films had nothing to do with the war. At the outbreak of hostilities two Hollywood films were playing in London which contributed songs that many people took to heart. Judy Garland's *Over the Rainbow* from the film 'The Wizard of Oz' and the cartoon character Jiminy Cricket's two songs *When You Wish Upon a Star* and *Give a Little Whistle* from Walt Disney's 'Pinocchio' proved enormously popular in the uncertainty of the Phoney War period.

When you get in trouble
And don't kmow right from wrong
Give a little whistle, toodeloo,
Give a little whistle, toodeloo.

The biggest-selling song of all time, *White Christmas*, was first performed by Bing Crosby in the 1942 classic 'Holiday Inn'. Towards the end of the war Judy Garland scored another winner with *The Trolley Song* from the film 'Meet Me in St Louis' while Dick Haymes had a winner in *The More I See You* from the film 'Diamond Horseshoe' just after VJ-Day in August 1945.

Films also gave fans a chance to see and hear some of the big-name American bands. In 1942 alone, for example, one could see Glenn Miller in 'Sun Valley Serenade', Jack Teagarden in 'Birth of the Blues', Jimmy Dorsey in 'The Fleet's In' and Gene Krupa in 'Ball of Fire'. Indeed, some films are remembered almost entirely for their music. In 'Dangerous Moonlight', Anton Walbrook starred as a Polish pianist who escaped from the Nazis only to lose his memory after flying in the Battle of Britain. His spirited play-ing of the *Warsaw Concerto* as the bombs rained down around him symbolized for many the spirit of resistance to Hitler. The music, by Richard Addinsell, helped bridge a culture gap. For many cinema-goers it was their first taste of 'classical' music and many elitists were as surprised then by its unexpected popularity as they were fifty years later when football crowds took the Italian operatic aria *Nessun Dorma* to heart.

JUDY GARLAND, IN A 1939 PUBLICITY SHOT FOR 'THE WIZARD OF OZ'.

From Swing to Symphony

Classical music in general reached new audiences during the war. Having been introduced to classical music, many people found that it touched deeper levels of emotion than some of the popular songs. Henry Wood's promenade concerts increased in popularity, and when their home in the Queen's Hall was bombed they relocated to the Albert Hall. The big-band leaders were not slow to pick up on the widening tastes in popular music. Glenn Miller added a twenty-one-instrument string section to his swing band. While in Britain they performed not only as an integral part of Miller's definitive AEF Orchestra, but also made radio broadcasts and concert appearances on their own under the name of Strings With Wings (Miller's wartime orchestra was formed, of course, under the command of the US army air force). In Britain, bandleader and impresario Jack Hylton also expanded the range of popular music. As early as the summer of 1940 he introduced the London Philharmonic Orchestra and the pianist Eileen Joyce to variety theatre audiences in Glasgow. The success of these and other experiments in serious music caused the more enterprising managements of variety theatres to provide more classical entertainment as part of their regular bill. Classical music entered the workplace through such BBC Radio programmes as 'Music While You Work' while ENSA presented special symphony concerts for war workers. The first of these was in Wigan, where John Barbirolli conducted the Hallé Orchestra. Confounding the sceptics (not the least of which were some of his own musicians) this concert was a great success and was followed by many more at locations around the country. Even before more serious music was taken to the workers, however, ENSA had begun providing classical music concerts for the troops. The first such concert was performed at the Garrison Theatre, Aldershot, in October 1940. The USO (United Services Organization), ENSA's American counterpart, similarly toured some of the great classical musicians. Pablo Casals was just one of the many luminaries who entertained the soldiers during the war.

The difficulties inherent in moving whole orchestras, as opposed to solo entertainers, limited to a certain degree the ability of ENSA or the USO to deliver live concerts to the far-flung fields of war. In any event, as the war progressed, the armed forces became more dispersed and travel became more difficult, even the movement of solo artists became difficult. As a result, both organizations became involved in ambitious recording programmes. These (V-Discs for the Americans, ORBS – Overseas Recorded Broadcast Service – for Britain) recorded on gramophone records the best popular and light classical music of the day for delivery to the troops.

About 20,000 ORBS sound recordings were made during the course of the war. They were organized by a government department, the Army Welfare Department, which established the ORBS both to cater to ENSA's recording needs and to co-ordinate the distribution of the finished

A lunchtime concert at the National Gallery with Miss (later, Dame) Myra Hess at the piano.

116

product. The recordings were made by top music and light entertainment artistes from both Britain and the Commonwealth who gave their services free of charge. A number of locations were used, including Basil Dean's HQ at the Theatre Royal, Drury Lane, and the Fortune Theatre. The sound was sent by land-line to EMI's Abbey Road studio where the records were processed. The pressings were all 12 in. 78s. Initially, they were made of shellac, but the high attrition rate caused by rough handling resulted in a shift to vinyl in later pressings. In the early days, the records had hand written lick-and-stick labels (few of which have survived to the present day). Later, circular labels bearing the legend 'ENSA Calling' and 'Services Calling' were used.

The finished gramophone records were distributed to special entertainment centres run for the servicemen where they were played through public-address systems or over the radio. In the simplest case, a single-speaker PA system would be mounted in a small van (the precursor of the mobile disco) which would travel to various troop centres where its operator, an amateur DJ, would play both the ENSA and commercially recorded material. At the other extreme, the discs were distributed to the forty-three radio stations from Iceland to Malaya for broadcast to troops in the field. The largest, the 100-kW medium-wave transmitter in Colombo, Ceylon, could reach listeners all round the Indian Ocean.

The fragility of the records, the scarcity of vinyl (many records were 'recycled' after a comparatively short life), and the fact that they were controlled by a quango mean that few have survived to the present day. The largest collection is held by the Imperial War Museum, where they are available only for research purposes. Those in the hands of private collectors are becoming valuable, but with so many lacking labels it must be assumed that there are many more sitting in lofts and garden sheds awaiting discovery.

The Americans ran a project similar to

Packing
ORBS gramophone records
for a mobile ENSA entertainment unit.

that of ORBS, issuing what were called V-(for 'Victory') Discs. These are extremely important as they are virtually the only records made by the top American performers during the American Federation of Musicians' recording ban (which ran from August 1942 to November 1944). Like the ORBS recordings, the V-Discs were 12 in. 78s. In most cases, each side contained two songs. Around twenty different V Discs were issued each month and a total of 8 million were distributed to GIs in the course of the war. (From mid-1944 to mid-1945 the Special Services division of the US army also distributed 125,000 gramophones to the troops.) They were sent out to camps, posts, ships, stations, and hospitals to be played over the PA systems M*A*S*H- style. Distributed with the discs would be the 'Army-Navy Hit Kit of Popular Songs' (special music sheets printed for the purpose). As the army moved forward, many of the recordings were left behind. Today, like ORBS recordings, they are increasingly collectable.

Although most of the music recorded on the ORBS and V-Discs came from the popular singers and bands of the day, there was also a significant amount of classical and light classical music as well. Toscanini and Arthur Rubinstein could be found rubbing shoulders, metaphorically at least, with Bing Crosby and the Andrews Sisters in V-Disc collections. The New York Philharmonic or the Boston Symphony could be found next to The Glenn Miller or the Duke Ellington Orchestras.

CHAPTER TWELVE

Victory

I'm Gonna Get Lit Up

ALTHOUGH THERE WERE many songs with the word 'victory' in the title – *When We Dance at the Victory Ball, Victory Waltz, Victory Polka* – comparatively few songs were actually written exclusively to celebrate the end of the war. Most victory songs were written well before the end of the war in Europe. There were several reasons for the lack of victory songs written around VE-Day. First, the government made a specific effort to tone down talk of victory during the spring of 1945. Fear of 'war fatigue' and faltering will when the end was in sight led to constant reminders through early 1945 that there was still a long way to go before the war was won. Thus, while it was allright to

TRAFALGAR SQUARE,
VE-DAY, 8 MAY 1945.
WRACs SHOW THE FLAG.

Victory

talk and sing of future victories in 1943 and 1944, by 1945 such sentiments were played down – except for a brief period of jubilation after the capitulation of Germany. The realization that there was no end in sight for the war in the East was a second reason. The tenacious last-ditch fighting by the Japanese cost the Allies dear for every piece of ground regained. The British advance overland through India and Burma and the Americans' 'island hopping' in the Pacific involved some of the most ferocious battles of the war.

On Monday 7 May 1945, Germany surrendered, and, at 7.30pm that evening, the news that the war in Europe was over was broadcast to the nation. It was also announced that Tuesday 8 May was to be a public holiday, VE-Day, to celebrate the victory in Europe. The response of the nation was, however, immediate and within minutes impromptu celebrations had begun.

Britain went barmy. The people of Glasgow were among the first off the mark as thousands thronged to George Square, where pipers were out in force. Other cities and towns across the land held their own, less riotous, celebrations. Flags waved, bonfires were lit, pubs stayed open till midnight and there was, quite literally, dancing in the streets.

Nowhere was the jubilation more intense than in London. By 9pm the streets of the West End were clogged with hundreds of thousands of civilians and servicemen. The celebrations soon spilled over into the Mall and a massive crowd converged on Buckingham Palace shouting for the King. There were huge

cheers as the King and Queen appeared on the balcony with their children, Elizabeth – still in her ATS uniform – and Margaret grinning madly at the vast crowds and waving their arms till they ached. The Royal Family was joined by Winston Churchill and it was only after midnight – and their eighth appearance on the balcony – that they were finally allowed to retire. The all-purpose party song *Knees Up Mother Brown*, first recorded by comediennes Gert and Daisy (Elsie and Doris Waters), was sung and danced to till the early-morning hours. But it was Hubert Gregg's *I'm Gonna Get Lit Up,* written back in 1943, that far more accurately described the mood of euphoria that night.

Lighting up of a different kind was a constant theme in the blacked-out war years. When these songs were first written they spoke of a time in the future when the irksome blackout

restrictions would be lifted and at the war's end they had a renewed burst of popularity.

The relaxation of blackout restrictions began well before the end of the war. The first stage took place on 17 September 1944. Under the new 'dim-out' conditions there was a partial return to normality as regular curtains replaced blacked-out windows in all but coastal areas. By the end of the year, normal lighting was again permitted for motor cars and on the railways, trams and buses, although it was not until 24 April 1945 that all lighting restrictions were rescinded. These changes brought a renewed vitality to such songs as *Till the Lights of London Shine Again* (1940) and *When the Lights Go on Again* (1942). While in America Duke Ellington and Harry James, perhaps coincidentally, celebrated the light at the end of the tunnel in their *I'm Beginning to See the Light.*

Meanwhile, for the American GIs, bands were playing the Glenn Miller swing version of the recycled American Civil War march *When Johnny Comes Marching Home*. Sadly, Glenn Miller himself was never to march again. His plane had been lost over the English Channel on 16 December 1944 whilst he was on

ONE OF THE THOUSANDS OF STREET PARTIES ENJOYED BY CHILDREN ALL OVER BRITAIN AFTER THE VICTORY IN EUROPE.

his way to conduct his band for the US forces in France.

Miller was undoubtedly one of the most memorable international casualties of the Second World War, but now his music lives on with millions of old and new fans alike. Only recently some new recordings have been found of him conducting probably his best-ever band in a session recorded at Abbey Road studios in St John's Wood, London, where, less than twenty years later, the Beatles recorded their greatest hits. These recordings – made of six propaganda broadcasts performed by the Miller orchestra and beamed to Germany – are, arguably, the definitive Miller sound. The orchestra was then at its peak of perfection. Only a few weeks after the recordings were made Miller died.

The Miller Orchestra, however, continued. Two of its members, Ray McKinley and Mel Powell, wrote a song of homecoming that was immensely popular in the US. Sung by Dinah Shore, *My Guy's Come Back* caught perfectly the mood of happy return after long years of separation and fear.

> *Somethin's cookin' that rates an ovation,*
> *Note that I'm in a state of elation,*
> *Call the press in, I've got a quotation,*
> *Tell the nation my guy's come back.*

A mood of a different sort was captured by Cole Porter, whose number-one hit coincided with the end of the war in Europe. Sung by Bing Crosby, his *Don't*

'DER BINGEL', COMPLETE WITH GERMAN HELMET, ENTERTAINS AT THE PIANO.

Fence Me In seemed to symbolize the idea that the world was now free from tyranny (not only of power-hungry dictators but also the soldier's desire to escape from military regimentation and the civilian's desire to see the back of wartime restrictions and rationing).

> *Oh give me land, lots of land,*
> *Under starry skies above,*
> *Don't fence me in.*
> *Let me ride thru' the wide open*
> *   country that I love,*
> *Don't fence me in.*
> *Let me be myself*
> *   in the evening breeze,*
> *Listen to the murmur of the cotton*
> *   wood trees,*
> *Send me off for ever, but I ask you please,*
> *Don't fence me in.*

Another song that will forever be associated with the end of the war in Europe is Ivor Novello's *We'll Gather Lilacs*. The song was from his hit show 'Perchance to Dream', which had opened at the London Hippodrome on 21 April 1945.

You Must Remember This...

THE SMILES SAY IT ALL. WINSTON CHURCHILL STANDS BETWEEN THE KING AND QUEEN, AND THE PRINCESSES ELIZABETH AND MARGARET, RESPONDING TO THE CROWDS OUTSIDE BUCKINGHAM PALACE ON VE-DAY.

It was first sung by the show's stars, Olive Gilbert and Muriel Barron, but was soon on everyone's lips.

We'll gather lilacs in the spring, again,
And walk together down an English lane
Until our hearts learned to sing again.
When you come home once more.

Other popular songs from this time – *I'm Going to Build a Future World Around You, When the Great New World is Dawning* – gave expression to the hopes for a better tomorrow.

People everywhere looked forward to the end of hostilities and anticipated its end long before the war was over. Hugh Charles and Louis Elton wrote *When They Sound the Last All-Clear* in the dark days of 1941. Yet the song expressed the heartfelt desire of everyone for the better days that would come after the last air-raid siren had been stilled. The lyric looks forward to the time when the blackout has ended and the dark lonely nights are only a memory before concluding:

For the peace bells will ring,
And the whole world will sing,
When they sound the last all-clear.

Frances Ash's *I'm Gonna Love That Guy (Like He's Never Been Loved Before)* revealed a more delicious anticipation:

I'm gonna love that guy like he's never
*   been loved before,*
I'm gonna show that guy he's the fella
*   I adore.*

But the war was not yet truly over. Although Rangoon had been taken on 2 May, the same day as the fall of Berlin, the war in the Pacific was to rage for another three months. As attention focused on the 'Forgotten 14th' (the biggest single army of the war) in its fight against Japan, entertainment also moved further afield. Although there had been

sporadic entertainment of the troops in Asia, logistical problems meant that this area was woefully underserved. ENSA made rapid moves to redeploy its troupes and by June 1945 there were over 250 ENSA artistes and over 150 local artistes at work in India and the Southeast Asia Command. Both the RAF and the Royal Marines posted their orchestras to the Far East and by August the first of 15,000 promised gramophones also arrived.

The atomic bombing of the Japanese cities of Hiroshima on 6 August 1945 and Nagasaki three days later brought the war to an abrupt end. The Japanese surrendered on 14 August, although owing for the need to synchronize the announcement between London, Washington, Moscow and Chungking (China's wartime capital), it was midnight before the victory could be announced. That announcement officially marked the end of the Second World War. The 15th and 16th of August were set aside as public holidays. Because of the lateness of the hour of announcement there were, unlike on VE-Day, relatively few unofficial celebrations, although the Glaswegians were again

quick off the mark. However, the lack of spontaneous rejoicing on the night of the 14th only served to make the official celebrations that began on the 15th the wildest the country had ever seen.

But although it was not until August 1945 that Japan finally capitulated, it had not stopped Britain from rejoicing on VE-Day. Flags and bunting and balloons lined every street in every town and village throughout the land, and street parties for the children with cakes and jellies appeared miraculously from nowhere (sugar was still rationed). And what did everyone continue to do? They sang the songs that had kept them going during the war, those five and a half long, dark years. The debt that is owed to those songwriters, singers, musicians and entertainers who helped to keep the morale in Britain so high through every phase of the worst war the world has ever known can never really be repaid.

But perhaps a special thanks can be made to them using the title of one of the most popular songs ever to be belted out from every barrack room in Britain –

Bless 'em all!

STAR PROFILES

Arthur ASKEY

'BIG-HEARTED' ARTHUR ASKEY was born in the docklands area of Liverpool on 6 June 1900. After serving in the army in the later stages of the First World War, Askey entered showbiz as a member of an 'End of the Pier' concert party troupe. He first became a household name as the star of Britain's first radio situation comedy, 'Band waggon', set in a fictional apartment on top of the BBC's Broadcasting House. During the war, Askey was in great demand on the Home Front, entertaining British servicemen at various training camps up and down the country. He was also a very popular recording artist, being the first singer to record *We're Gonna Hang Out the Washing on the Siegfried Line*. His recording of *Thanks for Dropping in Mr Hess* was briefly subjected to a government ban! He used to proclaim proudly that, because of his records and his initials, he was top of Hitler's Black List.

Arthur Askey introduces the 'Victory V-headed Calf' of the Red Cross Agricultural Fund to the stall holders of Covent Garden Market on 2 September 1942.

3 October 1941: Askey has a good look at his god-daughter, baby Linda, being held by her mother, Peggy Rawlings, while her father Richard 'Stinker' Murdoch, who is in the airforce, looks on.

Noël COWARD

NOËL COWARD was born in Teddington on 16 December 1899. He was nicknamed 'The Master' by his fellow artistes, and not surprisingly so, for it is doubtful if there has ever been a more versatile British creative talent. He was a prolific and highly successful playwright, composer, lyricist, actor, director, film star, producer and, in his middle years, one of the world's greatest cabaret performers. He was a friend of Royalty and in particular of Lord Louis Mountbatten, whose exploits were the inspiration of his Oscar-winning 1942 film *In Which We Serve*. Coward not only wrote a stream of witty patriotic songs, he travelled extensively on behalf

(Above)
Coward in a still from In Which We Serve and (left) during a moment between scenes, boarding HMS Torrin, the ship featured in the film.

of ENSA, performing everything from his idiosyncratic 'point numbers' to excerpts from his plays, and following with great enthusiasm the advice Winston Churchill had given to him at the commencement of the Second World War: 'Go and sing to them when the guns are firing – that's your job!'

STAR PROFILES

Bing CROSBY

'BING' CROSBY was born Harry Lillis Crosby in Tacoma, Washington, on 2 May 1901. At the age of eight he was given the nickname 'Bing' after a cartoon-strip character to whom he bore more than a passing resemblance. He first realized that he had a rather special singing talent when he was twelve years old and began impersonating his hero, Al Jolson, whom he had seen perform live on stage.

Crosby's first big break in show biz was when the self-styled 'King of Jazz', Paul Whitewan, signed him up to sing with his orchestra. In time he was given his own radio show and Hollywood soon beckoned. Crosby holds some astonishing 'records'. He has starred in more successful films than any other singer in the history of cinema; he has also sold more gramophone discs than any other artiste, including Elvis Presley and the Beatles. At the last count, in excess of 375 million of his records had been sold and that was for the Decca label alone. And his sales of the Irving Berlin composition *White Christmas* has sold well in excess of

Bing Crosby and Bob Hope performed many times together, both on screen and in the theatre.

thirty million copies, an accomplishment that is unlikely to ever be surpassed. With comedian Bob Hope, a golfing fanatic like himself, he made a series of 'road' movies that are now part of Hollywood legend. But his Academy Award (double) came when he picked up an Oscar for Best Actor in the 1944 film 'Going My Way', and was singer of the Oscar-winning song from the same film, written by Jimmy Van Heusen and Johnny Burke, called *Swinging On A Star*.

Crosby, persuaded at first by his screen partner Bob Hope, became a regular star performer on USO tours, where his relaxed, easy style and modesty made him an enormous favourite with US personnel. He always insisted that his audience should be comprised of all ranks from four-star generals to 'Buck' privates. In later years, the former 'enemy', Germany, adopted Bing and referred to him affectionately as 'Der Bingle'. For the rest of us, he will always be known by his self-styled put down, 'the old groaner'.

Bing Crosby in his most famous role, in the 1954 film 'White Christmas'.

STAR PROFILES

Gracie FIELDS

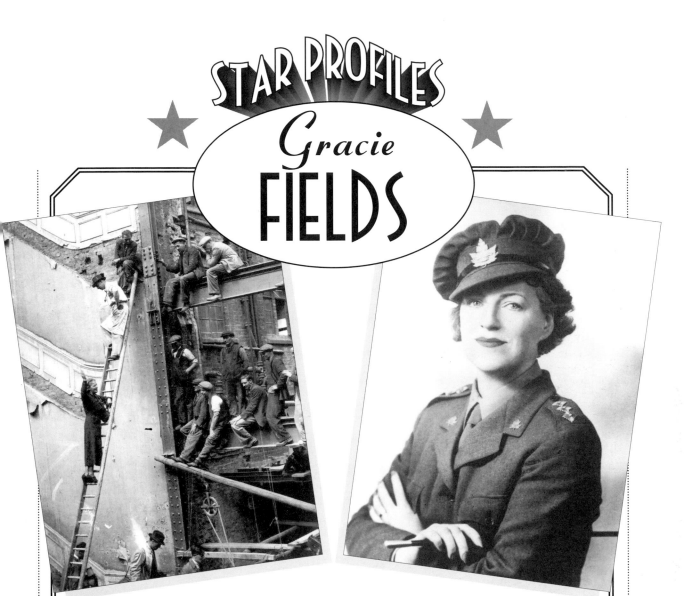

GRACIE FIELDS (GRACE STANSFIELD) was born in Rochdale, Lancashire, on 9 January 1898. She spent much of her childhood above her grandmother's fish and chip shop, where, encouraged by her mother, Jenny, she learned to sing and developed a unique comedic style. Her effervescent personality and Lancashire sense of humour made her a great favourite with theatre and film audiences during the Depression of the 1930s. She was Director of ENSA Basil Dean's first film-star choice to entertain the troops in France at the beginning of the war. Although her second husband, Monty Banks, an Italian-born British film director, was briefly threatened with internment as an

(Above) Gracie sings to the workmen at the laying of the foundation stone of the new Prince of Wales Theatre in London, in 1937.

enemy alien, Gracie still devoted much of her considerable energy to the Allied cause in the Second World War, travelling thousands of miles 'to cheer up the Lads' with her songs. She was especially admired by the Royal Family and holds the female record for her number of Royal Command appearances. She lived the last years of her life on the Isle of Capri with her third husband, Boris Alperovici.

STAR PROFILES

George FORMBY

GEORGE FORMBY was born in Wigan, Lancashire, on 26 May 1904. He was the son of the famous music hall comedian, George Formby Senior – 'the Wigan Nightingale'. George Formby Junior became Britain's most successful feature-film comedian and after marrying ex-dancer Beryl, who became his manager, mentor and female Zvengali, he was soon the highest-paid entertainer on stage and screen. It was she who dressed him in expensive lounge suits, silk shirts, hand-made shoes, no funny hats like all his contemporaries. George became a skilled banjo ukelele player which always featured prominently in his act, his films, and his best selling records. He was a tireless entertainer on behalf of ENSA and was highly critical of stars who had not given their services for the 'Boys' but instead stayed at home lining their pockets. There is a strong movement today to build a statue of him in his birth town of Wigan.

George and his wife, Beryl, leaving for France on 5 March 1940 to entertain the BEF.

Formby stars in the 1940 film, 'Let George Do It'.

ASSOCIATED TALKING PICTURES
Present

George FORMBY

LET GEORGE DO IT

PRODUCED *by* MICHAEL BALCON · DIRECTED *by* MARCEL VARNEL

STAR PROFILES

Judy GARLAND

JUDY GARLAND has been called 'the greatest female entertainer of them all'. This accolade comes not just from her millions of adoring admirers, but from her superstar peers, like Gene Kelly, who, whilst waiting for her to turn up in the long-delayed shooting of the movie 'Summer Stock' said: 'I don't care how long I wait for that girl – I'd wait forever for that magic.'

Judy was literally 'born in a trunk' backstage at the Princess Theatre – which her father managed – in Grand Rapids, Minnesota, on 10 June 1922. Her real name was Frances Gumm and she was the third member of a trio of daughters to singer Frank Gumm and pianist Ethel Milne - who had a double act they called 'Jack and Virginia Lee - Sweet Southern Singers'. She trod the boards herself as a singing, dancing toddler, and at the age of thirteen changed her name to Judy Garland, the forename being inspired by Hoagy Carmichael's hit song of the time, *Judy*.

Judy Garland and Mickey Rooney in a scene from the 1939 Busby Berkeley musical 'Babes in Arms'.

Judy Garland will always be, to everyone who recalls her name, the little girl Dorothy from the 1939 movie 'The Wizard of Oz'; and the hit song *Over the Rainbow* which won for its writers, Harold Arlen and E.Y. (Yip) Harburg, an Academy Award, will always be associated with her. The story behind this song goes that when an MGM executive watched the rough cut of the film, his comment to the director, Victor Fleming, was: 'The kids'll love it, but you gotta take that song out – it slows the movie down!' Luckily, Fleming didn't listen to his advice and it became Judy's most requested number. During the war, she continued to make some of the very best of Hollywood musicals, including the outstandingly successful 'For Me and My Girl (1942) and 'Meet Me in St Louis' (1944), which featured her second most popular number, *The Trolley Song*; and she was again instrumental in winning an Academy Award for its writers, Ralph Blane and Hugh Martin, by the sheer magic of her performance.

In 1969, just three years after her tragic death at the age of 47, her daughter, Liza Minelli, who has carried on with the family singing and dancing tradition, picked up an Oscar for her role as night club singer Sally Bowles in the movie 'Cabaret'. Judy's other daughter, Lorna Luft, also has a highly successful stage act, and both of these stars at some point in their stage performances, invariably include a medley of their mother's greatest hits.

STAR PROFILES

Bob HOPE

BOB HOPE (LESLIE TOWNES HOPF) was born in Eltham, a suburb of London, the fifth son of a stonemason, on 29 May 1903. When he was four his parents and their large family emigrated to Cleveland, Ohio, where he spent his early years. After leaving school, he tried his hand at several jobs from stockboy in a meat market to professional boxer. Eventually, he decided to go into showbiz after watching a performance of his idol, Charlie Chaplin – another London immigrant. He took dancing lessons from a black entertainer, King Rastus Brown, and embarked on a career as a song and dance man in Vaudeville. He began to introduce 'gag patter' into his act and headed towards Hollywood. His radio shows and feature films were to make him one of the greatest stars ever. No performer has ever travelled more than Hope to entertain the troops overseas, both in war and peacetime. Throughout the Second World War, the Korean War, the Vietnam War and in almost every US Service Base in Europe and the Far East Hope could

(Above) Bob Hope practises for a charity golf match with his longtime friend Bing Crosby and (left) meeting US soldiers with Frances Langford on a visit to London in June 1943.

be counted on to entertain the guys and gals. He has been a friend of US Presidents and played golf with most of them. To millions of Americans this master of the wisecrack is a national institution.

STAR PROFILES

Danny KAYE

DAVID DANIEL KAMINSKY was born in Brooklyn, New York, on 18 January 1913. He was the first American-born son of a Jewish Russian immigrant couple, Jakob and Clara Kaminsky. Danny grew up in the tough area of Brownsville, where some of his playmates were fully-fledged gang members of 'Murder Incorporated' and ended their young lives in the gas chamber of Sing Sing prison. The schoolboy David had ambitions to become a doctor, but the family never had enough money to send him to college. So, in his own words, 'I just drifted into show business', first as part of a two-part harmony act, then as the clown in a dancing trio which toured the Far East. Just before the outbreak of the war, he made his first trip to London to perform in cabaret as the stooge to a comedian called Nick Long at the Dorchester Hotel. The act was a disaster and the booking abruptly terminated. He went back to New York broke and despondent. Eventually he met Sylvia Fine, the daughter of a dentist for whom he had briefly run errands as a young boy. She was a pianist who specialized in writing zany point material. The pair clicked at first sight and soon Sylvia was writing tailored songs that would encompass Danny's enormous range of verbal virtuosity, from scat singing to satire. After a tour of the Catskill Mountains circuit of hotels, Danny was booked at

the New York Niterie La Martinique. He was a sensation. Ed Sullivan, who was there on opening night, wrote: 'I've never seen a star so completely fracture an audience'. On the strength of this success, Danny and Sylvia eloped and were married in Florida. Soon after this event, Danny was signed up by Hollywood mogul Sam Goldwyn and made a string of hit movies beginning in 1944 with 'Up In Arms'.

In between movies – like his great friends Frank Sinatra and Bob Hope – Kaye was an energetic entertainer on behalf of USO and toured thousands of miles to perform his unique act to the delight of service audiences. After the war, Kaye was booked at the London Palladium and became the greatest single sensation the world's most famous variety theatre had ever known. His seasons there are now part of show-biz mythology. He became firm friends with the young Princesses Elizabeth and Margaret as well as Sir Winston Churchill, Bernard Shaw, Laurence Olivier and a host of other British luminaries.

Sam Goldwyn said of Kaye: 'As a film comedian, he ranks alongside Chaplin and Keaton. As a stage entertainer – he stands alone'.

Danny Kaye with his wife, Sylvia Fine, at the Savoy Hotel in London, in November 1948.

STAR PROFILES
Vera LYNN

If ever there was a singer of popular songs whose name alone immediately evokes the music of the Second World War, that singer must surely be Vera Lynn. Even without mentioning the songs that will always be associated with her, like *We'll Meet Again* and *The White Cliffs of Dover*, for millions of people, Vera Lynn will have a permanent and special place in their hearts. Immediately after she starred in her 1941 radio series 'Sincerely Yours', she was dubbed 'The Forces Sweetheart', a term of endearment that remains with her to this day.

Vera Lynn – real name Vera Welch – was born in London on 20 March 1917. At the age of eleven she joined a theatrical group called Madam Harris's Kracker Kaberet Kids. She stayed with the 'Kids' for four years, then sang with a local band which led to a two-week gig with the Billy Cotton Band and an audition with Henry Hall and his Orchestra, resulting in one of her very few rejections. But the Henry Hall turn-down became Joe Loss's gain, for by 1935 she was a regular vocalist with his band. Also at this time, she often broadcast with pianist Charlie Kunz from the Casini Club, and it was with him that she made her first commercial record, *I'm in the Mood for Love*.

Vera Lynn gets a naval welcome as she arrives to sing in Trafalgar Square on 10 June 1943.

Vera joined Ambrose's Orchestra in 1937 and married the clarinetist from the band, Harry Lewis, who became her mentor and manager and they are still together fifty-eight years on. In showbiz, that is almost a record in itself.

But it was the soldiers of the British Expeditionary Force who really made her name. She was to them a musical bridge that linked them with their loved ones back home, and her melodious voice with its girlish catch in the throat was an enormous moral-booster; as were her 1944 ENSA tours in Burma. She was the first British singer to have a simultaneous number one hit record in Britain and the USA, a remarkable double, which she achieved with her multi-million seller *Auf Weidersehen Sweetheart*. In 1975 Vera was made a Dame of the British Empire.

STAR PROFILES

Anne SHELTON

At the tender age of twelve, Anne Shelton auditioned for Ambrose and went to work for him, rather than be evacuated with other London children during the war. Even at that age, she had a remarkably mature voice. Although Ambrose signed her up to a long-term contract, she had to complete two more years at school before she was officially permitted to join him as a full time professional. Her 'boss' Bert – as Ambrose was called by his fellow musicians – did release her, however, to sing seven special broadcasts with Glenn Miller when he came to Britain with his legendary AEF Band. In fact, so impressed was Major Miller with this 'kid' who was a 'world-class vocalist' that he invited her to continue working with him after the war, when he returned to the USA. Who knows what direction her career might have taken had Glenn Miller not died tragically early.

Anne Shelton was born in Dulwich on the 10 November 1927 and, by all accounts, she could sing almost before she could talk. She had many big wartime hit songs and made the first record of *Lilli Marlene* with Tommie Connors' English lyrics. It was a song she later adopted as her own signature tune when she became a solo singer and was given the first of many radio series. Although there was no real rivalry, between Vera Lynn and herself during the war, radio listeners tended to fall into two camps regarding these two foremost British vocalists. In retrospect, Vera Lynn was perhaps preferred by servicemen whilst Anne Shelton was just a crochet or two ahead with the home audience.

Bing Crosby picked up where Miller had left off, by insisting that she worked with him when he came to Britain on a USA forces morale-boosting tour in 1944. Eleven years after the war, in 1956, Anne had her biggest ever hit record, appropriately titled *Lay Down Your Arms* which reached No. 1 in the UK charts; and in 1961 she nearly repeated this success with another service-inspired song, *Sailor*.

Up until her death in 1994, Anne was always summoned to Clarence House on the Queen Mother's birthday to sing her favourite song *You'll Never Know (Just How Much I Love You)*. The lyric would have made a good epitaph for Anne herself, from a grateful British public who remember just how much she did to keep their spirits up during those dark years of the Second World War.

DISCOGRAPHY

There are many tape cassettes and CDs on the market that provide compilations of songs from the war years. Some of the best include those of the 'Happy Days' series produced by Conifer records:

You Must Remember This	CDHD/MCHD265/6
The Songs That Helped Win the War	CDHD/MCHD403
VE-Day – A Musical Celebration	CDHD/MCHD306/7
Wish Me Luck as You Wave Me Goodbye	CDHD/MCHD301
Calling All Workers	CDHD/MCHD302
Ma, I Miss Your Apple Pie	CDHD/MCHD303
You'd Be So Nice to Come Home To	CDHD/MCHD304

For Glenn Miller fans there is the marvelous double album of recently discovered wartime recordings, also on the Conifer label:

Glenn Miller – The Lost Recordings   CDHD/MCHD410/2

Songs from the Movies

Over the Rainbow – 'The Wizard of Oz'
When You Wish Upon a Star – 'Pinocchio'
It's Foolish But It's Fun – 'Spring Parade'
Kiss the Boys Goodbye – 'Kiss the Boys Goodbye'
Don't Sit Under the Apple Tree – 'Private Buckaroo'
They're Either Too Young or Too Old – 'Thank Your Lucky Stars'
A Tangerine – 'The Fleet's In'
You'll Never Know – 'Hello, Frisco, Hello'
I Couldn't Sleep a Wink Last Night – 'Higher and Higher'
Is You Is or Is You Ain't My Baby – 'Follow the Boys'
Ac-cen-tchu-ate the Positive – 'Here Come the Waves'
Boogie Woogie Bugle Boy of Company 'B' – 'Buck Privates'
Chattanooga Choo Choo – 'Sun Valley Serenade'
Yankee Doodle Dandy – 'Yankee Doodle Dandy'
White Christmas – 'Holiday Inn'
(I've Got a Girl in) Kalamazoo – 'Orchestra Wives'
Say a Prayer for the Boys Over There – 'Hers to Hold'
Swinging on a Star – 'Going My Way'
I'll Walk Alone – 'Follow the Boys'
Now I Know – 'Up in Arms'
The Trolley Song – 'Meet Me in St Louis'
You'd Be So Nice to Come Home To – 'Something to Shout About'

The recording industry was very different fifty years ago. The concept of the radio Hit Parade was not invented until after the war. Nor were gramophone record sales an accurate indicator of a song's popularity. (They would not be of much use since in the recording climate of the 1940s many different artists would record versions of the same song. Even so-called signature tunes would be 'covered' by several different singers or bands.) The most reliable indicator of a song's popularity actually comes from sheet music sales. The Music Publisher's Association produced a weekly list (the Blitz and V-bombs permitting) of the number of song-sheets sold. These, plus the BBC's records of the number of times a song was broadcast over the radio, can be used to compile a list of the top tunes of the war.

TOP WARTIME TUNES

1939

☆ HEAVEN CAN WAIT

☆ WISH ME LUCK AS YOU WAVE ME GOODBYE

☆ I'LL BE SEEING YOU

☆ WE'RE GONNA HANG OUT THE WASHING ON THE SIEGFRIED LINE

☆ SOMEWHERE IN FRANCE WITH YOU

☆ THERE'LL ALWAYS BE AN ENGLAND

☆ RUN, RABBIT, RUN!

☆ FRANKLIN D. ROOSEVELT JONES

☆ LORDS OF THE AIR

☆ WINGS OVER THE NAVY

☆ AN APPLE FOR THE TEACHER

☆ GOODNIGHT CHILDREN, EVERYWHERE

1940

☆ IT'S A HAP-HAP-HAPPY DAY

☆ IT'S A LOVELY DAY TOMORROW

☆ IN THE MOOD

☆ THE LADY IS A TRAMP

☆ WHERE OR WHEN

☆ GIVE A LITTLE WHISTLE

☆ I'VE GOT MY EYES ON YOU

☆ WE'LL MEET AGAIN

☆ CARELESS

☆ I'LL PRAY FOR YOU

☆ WHEN YOU WISH UPON A STAR

☆ (SOMEWHERE) OVER THE RAINBOW

☆ A NIGHTINGALE SANG IN BERKELEY SQUARE

☆ IN THE QUARTERMASTER'S STORES

☆ TILL THE LIGHTS OF LONDON SHINE AGAIN

☆ TIGGERTY-BOO

☆ OH! WHAT A SURPRISE FOR THE DUCE

1941

☆ ROOM FIVE HUNDRED AND FOUR
☆ THANKS, MR ROOSEVELT
☆ WHY DON'T WE DO THIS MORE OFTEN?
☆ THE LAST TIME I SAW PARIS
☆ LONDON PRIDE
☆ MY KATRINA
☆ RUSSIAN ROSE
☆ YOU STARTED SOMETHING
☆ KISS THE BOYS GOODBYE
☆ I DON'T WANT TO SET THE WORLD ON FIRE
☆ IT'S FOOLISH BUT IT'S FUN
☆ I YI, YI, YI, YI, LIKE YOU VERY MUCH
☆ HEY! LITTLE HEN

1942

☆ CHATTANOOGA CHOO CHOO
☆ (I'VE GOT A GAL IN) KALAMAZOO
☆ THE SAILOR WITH THE NAVY BLUE EYES
☆ THAT LOVELY WEEKEND
☆ IT COSTS SO LITTLE
☆ DO YOU CARE?
☆ JEALOUSY
☆ I DON'T WANT TO WALK WITHOUT YOU
☆ SOME SUNNY DAY (WE'LL MEET AGAIN)
☆ MA, I MISS YOUR APPLE PIE
☆ DON'T SIT UNDER THE APPLE TREE
☆ DEEP IN THE HEART OF TEXAS
☆ THE WHITE CLIFFS OF DOVER
☆ YOU ARE MY SUNSHINE
☆ MOONLIGHT BECOMES YOU
☆ WHEN THE LIGHTS GO ON AGAIN
☆ WHITE CHRISTMAS

1943

☆ THIS IS THE ARMY, MR JONES
☆ DON'T GET AROUND MUCH ANY MORE
☆ JOHNNY DOUGHBOY FOUND A ROSE IN IRELAND
☆ LILI MARLENE
☆ WHO WOULDN'T LOVE YOU
☆ THE SMITHS AND THE JONES
☆ AMERICAN PATROL
☆ MY BRITISH BUDDY
☆ DEARLY BELOVED

☆ YOU WERE NEVER LOVELIER
☆ YOU'D BE SO NICE TO COME HOME TO
☆ IT CAN'T BE WRONG
☆ EVERY NIGHT ABOUT THIS TIME
☆ AS TIME GOES BY
☆ ALL OR NOTHING AT ALL
☆ I'M GONNA GET LIT UP
☆ BE LIKE A KETTLE AND SING
☆ DER FÜHRER'S FACE
☆ PRAISE THE LORD AND PASS THE AMMUNITION

1944

☆ PAPER DOLL

☆ I HEARD YOU CRIED LAST NIGHT

☆ I NEVER MENTION HIS NAME

☆ I COULDN'T SLEEP A WINK LAST NIGHT

☆ A LOVELY WAY TO SPEND THE EVENING

☆ ROLL ME OVER

☆ SHOO SHOO BABY

☆ IS YOU IS OR IS YOU AIN'T MY BABY?

☆ NO LOVE, NO NUTHING

☆ DO NOTHING TILL YOU HEAR FROM ME

☆ TIME WAITS FOR NO-ONE

☆ LONG AGO AND FAR AWAY

☆ SHINE ON VICTORY MOON

☆ SWINGING ON A STAR

☆ I'LL GET BY

☆ IF YOU EVER GO TO IRELAND

☆ THE TROLLEY SONG

1945

☆ IT HAD TO BE YOU

☆ DON'T FENCE ME IN

☆ IT COULD HAPPEN TO YOU

☆ AC-CEN-TCHU-ATE THE POSITIVE

☆ I'M BEGINNING TO SEE THE LIGHT

☆ THE MORE I SEE YOU

☆ COMING HOME

☆ MY GUY'S COME BACK

☆ WE'LL GATHER LILACS

☆ THERE GOES THAT SONG AGAIN

Signature Tunes

Ambrose	When Day Is Done	Woody Herman	Woodchoppers' Ball
Count Basie	One O'Clock Jump	Bob Hope	Thanks for the Memory
Les Brown	Sentimental Journey	Hutch	Begin the Beguine
Nat 'King' Cole	Straighten Up and Fly Right	Harry James	Ciribiribin
Billy Cotton	Somebody Stole My Gal	Charlie Kunz	Clap Hands, Here Comes Charlie
Jimmy Dorsey	So Rare		
Tommy Dorsey	I'm Getting Sentimental Over You	Joe Loss	In the Mood
		Vera Lynn	Yours
Duke Ellington	Take the 'A' Train	Glenn Miller	Moonlight Serenade
Gracie Fields	Sally	The Mills Bros.	Paper Doll
George Formby	Leaning on a Lamppost	Ray Noble	Goodnight, Sweetheart
Carroll Gibbons	On the Air	Harry Roy	Bugle Call Rag
		Maurice Winnick	The Sweetest Music This Side of Heaven

SELECT BIBLIOGRAPHY

Algate, Anthony and Jeffrey Richards, *Britain Can Take It*, Basil Blackwell, 1986

Askey, Arthur, *Before Your Very Eyes*, Woburn, 1975.

BBC Yearbooks, 1939–46.

Beaumont, Winifred, *A Detail on the Burma Front*, BBC Books, 1977.

Briggs, S., *Keep Smiling Through*, Fontana, 1976.

Butcher, Geoffrey, *Next to a Letter from Home: Glenn Miller's Wartime Band*, Mainstream, 1986.

Calder, Angus, *The People's War*, Jonathan Cape, 1969.

Colin, Sid, *And the Bands Played On*, Elm Tree, 1977.

Costello, John, *Love, Sex and War*, Collins, 1985.

Cotterell, Anthony, *RAMC*, Hutchinson, 1945.

Cotton, Billy, *I Did It My Way*, Harrap, 1956.

Coward, Noël, *The Lyrics of Noël Coward*, William Heinemann, 1965.

Coward, Noël, *Middle East Diary*, 1945.

Crowther, Bruce, Mike Pinfold and Franklin S. Driggs, *The Big Band Years*, David and Charles, 1988.

Dahl, Linda, *Stormy Weather*, Quartet, 1984.

Dance, Stanley, ed., *Jazz Era: The Forties*, MacGibbon & Kee, 1961.

Dean, Basil, *The Theatre at War*, Harrap, 1956.

Dougall, Robert, *In and Out of the Box*, Collins & Havrill, 1973.

Falk, Quentin, *The Golden Gong*, Columbus, 1987.

Fawkes, Richard, *Fighting For A Laugh*, Macdonald and Jane's, 1978.

Fields, Gracie, *Sing As We Go*, Frederick Muller, 1960.

Fisher, John, *George Formby*, Woburn-Futura, 1975.

Gifford, Denis, *Bless 'Em All*, Webb & Bower, 1989.

Grenfell, Joyce, *Entertaining the Troops*, Macmillan, 1990.

Grenfell, Joyce, *Requests the Pleasure*, Macmillan, 1976.

Harris, John, *A Funny Place to Hold a War*, Hutchinson, 1984.

Harrison, T., *Living Through the Blitz*, Collins, 1976.

Hawkins, Jack, *Anything for a Quiet Life*, Elm Tree, 1973.

Huggett, F.E., *Goodnight Sweetheart*, W.H. Allen, 1979

Hughes, John Craven, *Grease Paint War*, New English Library, 1976.

Ingersoll, R., *Report on England*, Right Book Club, 1941.

Jackson, Arthur, *The World of Big Bands: The Sweet and Swinging Years*, David & Charles, 1977.

Jacob, Naomi, *Me, Over There*, Hutchinson, 1947.

Jenkins, Alan, *The Forties*, Heinemann, 1977.

Johnson, S.B., ed., *The Evacuees*, Gollancz, 1968.

Kimball, Robert, *The Complete Lyrics of Cole Porter*, Vintage Books, 1983.

Lawrence, Gertrude, *A Star Danced*, W.H. Allen, 1945.

Leich, Michael, *World War II Songs*, Longmans, *Chronicle of the Second World War*, Longmans, 1990.

Longmate, Norman, *How We Lived Then*, Hutchinson, 1974.

Longmate, N., *The Real Dad's Army*, Hutchinson, 1974.

Lowe, Leslie, *Directory of Popular Music*, Waterlow, 1992.

Lynn, Vera, *Vocal Refrain*, W.H. Allen, 1975.

McCarthy, Albert, *Big Band Jazz*, Barrie & Jenkins, 1974.

McCarthy, Albert, *The Dance Band Era*, Studio Vista, 1971.

Maclean, Ian, *Ministry of Morale*, Allen & Unwin, 1979.

Marwick, A., *The Home Front*, Thames and Hudson, 1976.

Orwell, George, 'Letter from England' in the *Partisan Review*, 3 January 1943.

Page, Martin, *Kiss Me Goodnight, Sergeant Major,* Granada, 1973.

Pedrick, Gale, *Battledress Broadcasters*, British Forces Broadcasting Service, 1964.

Pertwee, Bill, *Stars in Battle Dress*, Hodder & Stoughton, 1992.

Purser, Philip and Jenny Wilkes, *The One and Only Phyllis Dixie*, Futura, 1978.

Rust, Brian, *The Dance Bands*, Ian Allen, 1972.

Simon, George T., *Glenn Miller and His Orchestra*, W.H. Allen, 1974.

Sunday Pictoral, *Sweethearts All*, 1945.

Taylor, Eric, *Showbiz Goes to War*, Robert Hale, 1992

Warren, Patricia, *Elstree – The British Hollywood*, Elm Tree, 1983.

Way, Chris, *The Big Bands Go to War*, Mainstream, 1991.

Wicks, B., *The Day They Took the Children*, Bloomsbury, 1989.

CHILDREN'S BOOKS

Cross, R., *Cities at War*, Wayland, 1994.

Rawcliffe, M., *Britain at War*, B.T. Batsford, 1992.

Ross, S., *The Home Front*, Wayland, 1990.

Wood, T. and R.J. Unstead, *The 1940s*, Franklin Watts, 1990.

For those who want to sing and play along, there are several collections of wartime music and lyrics available in good music shops. Among the best are the 'Seventy Years of Popular Music' series published by IMP (International Music Publications) of Woodford Green, Essex. Music books in this series include:

> *The Forties*, Parts 1, 2 and 3
> *The War Years*
> *The Big Band Era*.

Other IMP music books featuring songs from the war years include:

> *Take It Easy – The Forties*
> *I'll Be Seeing You*.

SONG INDEX

TITLES, COMPOSERS, YEAR OF PUBLICATION AND PUBLISHERS OF SONGS APPEARING IN THE TEXT.

A Fellow on a Furlough, Bobby Worth, 1943, ©Leonard-Worth Songs, *99*.

A Pair of Silver Wings, Michael Carr/Eric Mashwitz, 1941, ©Peter Maurice Music Co, *18*.

A Slip of the Lip (Can Sink a Ship), Mercer Ellington/©Luther Henderson, 1942, Edwin H. Morris Co., *52*.

Ac-cen-tchu-ate the Positive, Johnny Mercer/©Harold Arlen, 1944, Edwin H. Morris and Co., *135, 137*.

Adolf, Annette Mills, 1937, ©EMI Music Publishing Ltd, *13*.

Ain't Misbehavin', Andy Razaf/Thomas Waller/Harry Brooks, 1929, ©Lawrence Wright Music Co., *98*.

All Over the Place, Noel Gay/Frank Eyton, 1941, ©Noel Gay Music Co., *18*.

American Patrol, F.W. Meacham, 1981 (1943), ©Keith Prowse Music Publishing Co., *101*.

And the Angels Sing, Johnny Mercer/Ziggy Elman, 1939, ©Francis, Day and Hunter Ltd, *9*.

Bless 'Em All, Jimmy Hughes/Frank Lake, 1941, ©Keith Prowse Music publishing Co., *23*.

Blitzkrieg Baby, Fred and Doris Fisher, 1940, ©Fisher Music Corp., *57-58, 61*.

Boomps-a-Daisy, Annette Mills, 1939, ©Lawrence Wright Music Co., *12, 60*.

Brother There's a Job to Do, Mark Hess/Earl Robinson, 1942, ©T.B. Harms Co., *19*.

Bugle Call Rag, Elmer Schoebel/Bill Meyers/Jack Pettis, 1924, ©Lawrence Wright Music Co., *101*.

Bye Bye Benito, Lew Brown, 1942, ©Shapiro, Bernstein and Co., *28*.

Charlie, Joseph Mosbacher, 1943, ©Kelton Rom., *19*.

Chattanooga Choo Choo, Mack Gordon/Harry Warren, 1942, ©Robbins Music Corp. Ltd, *101*.

Chew-Chew-Chew (Your Bubble Gum), Buck Ram/Chick Webb/Ella Fitzgerald, 1939, ©American Academy of Music, Inc., *9*.

Cleanin' My Rifle and Dreaming of You, Allie Wrubel, 1943, ©Southern Music Publishing Company, *69*.

Colonel Bogey, Kenneth J. Alford, 1914, ©Boosey and Hawkes, *15*.

Concerto for Two, Jack Lawrence, 1941, ©Shapiro, Bernstein and Co.,

Conscription Waltz, J.P. Fox/Maurice Roffman, 1940, ©A-1 Music Publishing, *19*.

Could You Please Oblige Us with a Bren Gun?*, Noël Coward, 1940, ©Chappell and Co., *41*.

Crash! Bang! I Want to Go Home, Butler-Parr Davis, 1939, ©Chappell and Co., *35, 55*.

Dear Dark Eyes (adapted from the traditional Russian Hortche Chornye) Peter Kane, 1942, ©W. Paxton and Co. Ltd, *67*.

Deep in the Heart of Texas, June Hershey/Don Swander, 1942, ©Southern Music Publishing Co. Ltd, *101*.

Deep Purple, Peter De Rose/Mitchell Parish, 1939, ©Robbins Music Corp. Ltd.

Der Führer's Face, Oliver Wallace, 1943, ©Southern Music Publishing Co. Ltd *14*.

Do Nothing Till You Hear From Me, Bob Russell/Duke Ellington, 1943, ©Robbins Music Corp., *137*.

Don't Fence Me In*, Cole Porter, 1944, © Harms Inc., USA, Chappell and Co., *121, 137*.

Don't Get Around Much Any More, Bob Russell/Duke Ellington, 1942, ©Robbins Music Corp., *136*.

Don't Let's Be Beastly to the Germans*, Noël Coward, 1943, ©Chappell and Co., *49, 92*.

Don't Sit Under the Apple Tree, Sammy Stept/Charles Tobias/Lew Brown, 1942, ©Robbins Music Corp. Ltd, *99-100*.

Even Hitler Had a Mother, Herbert Farjeon/John Pritchett, 1939, ©Ascherberg, Hopwood and Crew Ltd, *12-13, 14, 94*.

Faithful Forever, Leo Robin/Ralph Rainger, 1939, ©Victoria Music Co. Ltd, *98*.

Fall In, Welcome, Lewis/Milton Shaw, 1941, ©Broadcast Music Inc., *19*.

Follow the White Line, ©Burnaby/North, *36*.

Four Buddies, Paul Cunningham/Leonard Whitcup, 1943, ©Broadway Music Corp., *19*.

(When the Lads of the Village) Get Crackin',

* extended lyrics for these songs are reproduced by permission of International Music Publications Ltd.
† extended lyrics for these songs are ©Noel Gay Music Co. Ltd.

(For any further information on any of the titles listed in this index, please contact The Performing Right Society, tel: 0171 580 5544).

You Must ★ Remember This...

IF YOU WOULD LIKE to
order the Compact Disc or Cassette
that accompanies the television programme and this book
please contact:

Summit Marketing
PO Box 554
HIGH WYCOMBE
Bucks HP12 4NH

Postal orders/cheques made payable to
Summit Marketing.
Major credit cards welcome.

Phone: 01494 - 471150
Fax: 01494 - 441498

Double CD	-	£13.99	(CDHD 265/6)
Double Cassette	-	£9.99	(MCHD 265/6)
Postage & Packing - £1.50 per order			